Another 100 Questions Ever
Know: ASWB-LCSW Exam P

MW00769044

Volume II

Another 100 Questions Every Social Worker Should Know: ASWB-LCSW Exam Preparation Guide

Volume II

Harvey Norris, MSW, LCSW

TURTLE PRESS

Library of Congress Cataloging in Publication Data

Norris, Harvey S.

ACKNOWLEDGEMENTS

This book is dedicated to my friend,
James V. Cook, ESQ
If the practice of law had not grabbed him, he would
have made a great social worker.

He sees the good in everyone, even those who appear
to be his adversaries. He has taught me about human
nature and how to fight better.

...and how not to carry a grudge...

Thank you for every breakfast...and every chance to do
good...

CONTENTS

101	and tells them she is a lesbian	Psychotherapy
102	motor skills are delayed	Psychotherapy
103	Jayne's parents divorced 18 months ago	Psychotherapy
104	none of your co-workers …is going to be in the building	Ethical
105	he wanted to confirm the time of his wife's appointment	Ethical
106	Psychosis is defined as a person	Clinical
107	Negative Symptoms are…	Clinical
108	during the night THEY come and rearrange all the bones in my face while I sleep	Clinical
109	When dealing with psychosis	Clinical
110	In order to properly diagnose Schizophrenia	Clinical
111	In the diagnosis of Schizophrenia	Clinical
112	John has withdrawn from his social circles…	Clinical
113	19-year-old male with a diagnosis of Schizophrenia	Clinical
114	You are reviewing a chart	Clinical
115	the word mood is used to describe	Clinical
116	A BIPOLAR DISORDER is a	Clinical
117	What is the difference between	Clinical
118	After an intensive interview with several members of the family	Clinical
119	you are dealing with a Mood Disorder	Clinical
120	Which of the following disorders can present	Clinical
121	you honor and respect the	Cultural

differences between cultures

122	who has been assigned to see a Guatemalan immigrant	Cultural
123	they are seeing you because their son is GAY	Cultural
124	a case involving an Asian-American youth	Cultural
125	You are asked to assess a man from New Guinea	Cultural
126	you realize her guilt is related to spending so much on tuition and	Clinical
127	on a 36 year old Arab-American	Clinical
128	on a 22 year old female whose parents are very concerned	Clinical
129	He is convinced that most people dislike him	Clinical
130	Juan and Isobel come to their first couple's session	Clinical
131	rather consistent with attending sessions	Clinical
132	You have developed an eco-diagram	Clinical
133	Tommy's parents say he just sits around	Clinical
134	You have taken a job as a prison social worker	Clinical
135	a 35 year old male who has served two brief prison terms	Clinical
136	You have completed your MSW	Ethical
137	You are hospital social worker in charge of discharge planning	Ethical
138	sessions to a 23 -year-old female client, who is indigent and has a nine month old baby boy	Ethical
139	insurance has authorized two sessions for assessment	Ethical
140	You are a hospice social worker	Clinical
141	You would be able to estimate his FSIQ	Clinical

142 therefore is more sensitive, more creative and more emotional	Clinical
143 she recently went to the doctor and he gave her an EEG	Clinical
144 You are seeing Sylvia for anxiety and depression	Clinical
145 they exhibit a belief of a "hands-off" attitude	Clinical
146 She appears delusional and disorganized	Human Diversity
147 The stage of the school age child is the	Clinical
148 You are working with an inter-generational family	Clinical
149 a 47 year old white female who is characteristically very shy	Clinical
150 One of the most powerful ethical cases	Ethics
151 she has been diagnosed with Borderline Personality Disorder	Clinical
152 he wishes he could understand the ONTOGENESIS	Clinical
153 His history is unremarkable before his current symptoms	Clinical
154 she is unable to afford the fees for therapy	Ethics
155 of sexual abuse by her stepfather	Clinical
156 diagnosed with a dysthymic disorder	Clinical
157 explain the difference between post-traumatic stress disorder	Clinical
158 He initially presented with moderate to severe depression	Clinical
159 You are supervising an intake worker at a	Clinical
160 One of your ethical commitments that is implicit in the NASW Code	Ethics
161 Your level of concern about their potential to commit suicide should	Clinical
162 who is diagnosed with a Bipolar Disorder	Clinical

163	a 43 year old female with a long history of chronic alcoholism	Clinical
164	referral reports problems with reality testing	Clinical
165	seeing a 23 year old female client who appears rather manipulative	Clinical
166	Each time the child begins to express emotions	Clinical
167	white male with an alcoholic wife who	Clinical
168	clients who suffer from drug or alcohol addiction	Clinical
169	Substance Abuse programs that use cognitive behavioral	Clinical
170	Of the four common groups of medications taken	Clinical
171	an intake for a court ordered client.	Psychothx
172	You are working with a client in a hospital	Ethics
173	when you can break confidentiality and disclose confidential	Ethics
174	You run into the client and learn they are a gardener and	Ethics
175	you decide the family is not appropriate for family therapy	Psychothx
176	Incest and family dynamics have several	Clinical
177	she spends entire days in her pajamas	Psychothx
178	Children reared in family environments	Psychothx
179	diagnosed with an anxiety disorder and an alcohol use disorder	Clinical
180	You have decided to administer the "Draw-a-Person" test	Diagnosis
181	states she is frustrated, overwhelmed and feels like she is drowning	Psychothx
182	There are many different theories for intervention	Psychothx
183	Of the four following childhood behaviors	Behavior

184 A repetitive and persistent pattern of behavior   Behavior

185 mother has just brought her eight year old boy   Diagnosis

186 You are completing the first session with a women   Psychothx

187 views a patient with unexpressed guilt as   Psychothx

188 The client's mother was killed in a single car accident   Psychothx

189 A cognitive bias is a pattern   Psychothx

190 have started an admission on a 38 year-old female client   Psychothx

191 lists a series of diagnoses which can only be used with children under the age of 18   Diagnosis

192 for personality disorders and mental Retardation   Diagnosis

193 Psychoanalytic theory postulates   Diagnosis

194 All other countries use the International   Diagnosis

195 working with a client who has a full scale IQ   Diagnosis

196 with a child who has been diagnosed with a conduct disorder   Diagnosis

197 who is described as "latency aged".   Diagnosis

198 issues including anger, aggression, and impulse control   Ethics

199 As an emergency room social worker   Diagnosis

200 You begin to explain confidentiality for   Assessment

Question 101   Section: Psychotherapy

A 19-year-old girl, upon returning from her first year away at college sits her parents down and tells them she is a lesbian. She tells them she has known of her orientation since she was 16 but has been afraid to tell them until now. The family normally has good relations and treats each other well. Her mother and father are angry, embarrassed and confused. Both parents feel disappointed in their daughters' orientation, embarrassed by her revelation and unsure of how to deal with her situation. Although the family typically gets along well, they are angry, confused, and embarrassed. Her father feels alienated from his daughter, and neither parent feels able to express their feelings about their daughter's sexuality nor their disappointment in her. Mother indicates that her husband has confided in her that he feels he is to blame because he was strict with her dating during high-school. How could you best help this family?

A) offer the girl and her family access to a re-orientation program in order to alter her sexual orientation.
B) Provide the girl with individual therapy to deal with her feelings about her orientation.
C) Provide crisis counseling to the family and refer the mother and father to a support group for parents of gay and lesbian children.
D) Educate the parents about the homosexuality and address their prejudices in a direct, blunt manner.

Answer on Page: 74

Question 102   Section: Psychotherapy

You have been referred a case of a seven year old boy. He has been tested and is in the low-average range of intellectual functioning. His motor skills are delayed and while he is able to walk between objects he often refuses to stand and pulls himself across the floor. The referral is due to risk of self harm because he persistently eats sand, bugs, houseplants, paint, dog food and has recently been caught eating cat feces from the cat litter box. He started this behavior four months ago and it has been continuous since. His primary diagnosis would MOST likely :

A) mental retardation
B) encopresis.
C) Asperger's
D) Pica

Answer on Page: 76

Question 103   **Section: Psychotherapy**

Jayne's parents divorced 18 months ago, after 2 years of almost constant daily bickering, when she was 14 years old. She lives with her mother and has started staying out all night, has come home drunk several times and has been caught smoking pot with her friends at least twice. Both mom and dad are upset about the behavior. Since she lives with mom, dad feels left out and unable to help his daughter. They come in to see you together and it is clear they are still grieving over the loss of their marriage, and they feel guilty because they blame the constant arguing that occurred before their divorce as the starting point for their daughter's rebellion. Both are concerned their daughter will continue to get in trouble and may end up in the legal system.
You have been seeing the daughter at school for a behavioral referral from a teacher. What would be your best option going forward?

A) Attempt to get Jayne involved in different after-school activities with the opportunity to meet and get involved with a different peer group.
B) Continue individual therapy with Jayne and provide and referrals to support groups and provide linking services
to   them for the parents dealing with the after-effects of divorce and co-parenting issues.
C) Continue individual therapy and tell the parents this is a stage that Jayne will mature out of.
D) Refer Jayne to a church youth group so she can develop a new set of friends.

Answer on Page: 78

Question 104   **Section: ETHICS**

You are a new female social worker at a mental health center. You have scheduled a client for tomorrow at 8 PM when you realize that none of your co-workers or your supervisor is going to be in the building. You have never met with this client and it will be your initial screening and interview. Your best course of action is to:

A) talk to your co-workers and ask if they can stay late that night so you are not alone.
B) Call the client and reschedule for a time when there are other people in the office.
C) Don't worry about the situation and see the client alone as scheduled.
D) Call your significant other and ask them if they can stay in the office waiting room while you see your client.

Answer on Page: 80

Question 105   Section: ETHICS

You have an appointment with Margaret scheduled for the evening. You receive a call from her husband around 3 in the afternoon, stating he wanted to confirm the time of his wife's appointment for her. You just attended training on HIPAA awareness. You should...

A) Tell the husband you cannot answer the question and then call Margaret and verify she asked her husband to confirm the appointment.
B) Ask the husband why he is calling instead of Margaret.
C) Let the husband know the time of the appointment so he can make sure Margaret is on time.
D) Refuse to acknowledge that Margaret is your client and refuse to discuss any appointment times with the husband.

Answer on Page: 81

Question 106   Section: CLINICAL

Psychosis is defined as a person who is out of touch with reality. There are five basic types of symptoms that define psychosis. If a person exhibits one or more of these symptoms you can say they are suffering from psychosis and then if you gather enough information you can arrive at a more exact diagnosis, e.g. Schizophrenia, Schizophreniform... Which of the following is NOT a symptom of PSYCHOSIS?

A) Delusions
B) Negative Symptoms
C) Alopecia
D) Disorganized Speech

Answer on Page: 82

Question 107   **Section: CLINICAL**

Negative Symptoms are one of the major symptoms of psychosis. A person with negative symptoms will often present with a FLAT or BLUNTED affect. They are called negative symptoms because...

A) they are characterized by a reduction in amount and fluency of speech.
B) They give the impression something has been taken away from the client.
C) they reduce the apparent TEXTURAL RICHNESS of a patient's personality.
D) All of the above

Answer on Page: 82

Question 108   **Section: CLINICAL**

Once during the beginning of my career, as I sold my time to an inpatient psychiatric facility for $4.97 per hour, I walked into the dayroom to find a male client, approximately 55 years of age sitting on a couch and pushing on his face from different angles. As I watched, he pushed harder and harder from different directions and seemed perplexed. I approached him and asked him how he was doing. He replied, "OK, I guess." And continued to touch his face. I then asked him what he was doing and he replied that he was making sure his face was all right? I commented that his face appeared fine and he said, "Now it does, but during the night THEY come and rearrange all the bones in my face while I sleep and I have to make sure they get them back in the right places!" Trying not to react strongly, I said, "That must be kind of painful!" He replied, "Not really, unless I wake up while they are doing it!" This client was experiencing a

A) Disorganized thought
B) A False Belief
C) Hallucination
D) Bizarre Delusion

Answer on Page: 83

Question 109   **Section: CLINICAL**

When dealing with psychosis, in order to diagnose correctly, you must look at longitudinal factors and associated disorder features. Which of the following is NOT a factor used to assist with diagnosis:

A) Duration of symptoms
B) Precipitating Factors of illness
C) Premorbid Personality
D) Previous employment history.

Answer on Page: 84

Question 110   **Section: CLINICAL**

In order to properly diagnose schizophrenia, it is important that the patient's occupational and social functioning be materially impaired. For example a person with this diagnosis would not be likely to marry or be in an intimate relationship (Material Social Impairment) and would not likely be able to hold a job (Material Occupational Impairment). Once you have determined that a person has PSYCHOSIS, you must then exclude other issues. PSYCHOSIS alone is not enough to diagnose schizophrenia. Which of the following would NOT be an exclusionary factor?

[15]

A) Substance Abuse Disorders
B) Mood Disorders
C) Family Illness
D) General Medical Condition

Answer on Page: 85

Question 111   Section: CLINICAL

In the diagnosis of schizophrenia, there are other features which need to be considered in order to properly complete the differential diagnosis. Which of the following features need to be considered...

A) Family History of Illness
B) Age of onset of illness
C) Response to Medications
D) All of the above

Answer on Page: 86

Question 112   Section: CLINICAL

John has withdrawn from his social circles and has begun to display rather peculiar habits when his friends come over to visit. All of his friends notice small behavior changes which include odd statements, reference to things that "cannot be" and comments regarding his belief's that his dog may be listening into his telephone conversations. He is not known to use any drugs and has had no medical history. Because John is mild mannered and pleasant, his friend have felt his behavior is odd but not a major concern. When Cecelia went to visit him yesterday, he had not bathed in several days. His bird feeder was removed from the backyard and was sitting on the table. When she asked about it he smiled pleasantly and said in a calm tone of voice, "The birds have been gathering around the bird feeder in order to spy on me and watch what I do during the day. So, I took down the birdfeeder so they can't come around anymore." He mentioned that he was happy because his brother started to call him again and they had a great conversation on the telephone that lasted for about an hour this morning. Cecelia knows that John had only one brother and he died in a car crash several years ago. Cecelia reported this to her friends and is very concerned. She calls a social worker she knows from work and they recommend John be evaluated for a psychotic disorder. Her social worker friend tells her that it is possible John is suffering from Schizophrenia. Cecelia goes online and learns the following about the onset of schizophrenia:

A) It affects about 5% of the population and once treated with medications the person should have no further problems.
B) It affects about 5% of the populations and most people continue to have symptoms throughout their lives.
C) It affects about 1% of the population and treatment is often provided using neuroleptic medications which can cause Tardive Dyskinesia and may have to be taken on a lifelong basis.
D) It affects about 1% of the population and can cause some incapacity of social and work functioning, but the functioning incapacity is seldom profound.

Answer on Page: 86

Question 113   Section: CLINICAL

You are dealing with Michael, a 19-year-old male with a diagnosis of Schizophrenia. Among all the symptoms he presents with, you notice the most prominent are the material impairment of his ability to socialize with other people and his inability to study his texts for his college courses. He is very distractible and at times can become disoriented as to his place and time, although this usually fades after 20-25 minutes. This constellation of behaviors is grouped under the psychotic symptom label of:

A) Absence of Insight
B) Cognitive dysfunction
C) Dysphoria
D) None of the above

Answer on Page: 87

Question 114   Section: CLINICAL

You are reviewing a chart for a client you are about to start seeing and you read the following diagnostic classification:

Axis I   295.60 Schizophrenia, Residual Type, Episodic With Interepisode Residual Symptoms.

What behavior would you expect to see in this individual?

A) A client who is primarily mute, with catalepsy (when some moves a client's body part, like raising their hand above their head – it will stay in the same position for several minutes)
B) A patient who would present with no impulse control problems, fully oriented and without suicidal ideations, and would be able to describe her most scary experiences with the same emotional tone as she would use for describing her dishes.

C) A patient who will present as appropriate but can deteriorate rapidly, talk gibberish, neglect their appearance and neglect their hygiene.

D) a patient who presents with a reduced or attenuated psychotic   symptoms such as odd speech or peculiarities of behavior that exist but are rather slight in presentation.

Answer on Page: 88

Question 115   Section: CLINICAL

In clinical parlance, the word mood is used to describe "a sustained emotion that colors the way we look at life". We used to use the term AFFECTIVE DISORDER instead of MOOD DISORDER, so be careful when reading older reports or talking to clinicians who received their initial training in the seventies and eighties, as they may use AFFECTIVE to mean MOOD. Which of the following facts are true about mood disorders?

A) Their prevalence is about 20% among adult females and 10%   among adult males
B) They occur regardless of social class and race
C) They are more common among single adults
D) All of the above

Answer on Page: 89

Question 116   Section: CLINICAL

A BIPOLAR DISORDER is a shorthand way of describing any cyclic mood disorder that includes at least one MANIC Episode. A MANIC Episode consists of a classic triad of symptoms (1) heightened self-esteem, (2) increased motor activity, and (3) pressured speech. Symptoms must be obvious and outrageous. You receive a patient with a diagnosis of 296.0

Bipolar Disorder, Single Manic Episode. Which of the following items can you infer from this diagnosis?

A) The patient has had AT LEAST one manic episode and one major depressive episode in the past.
B) The patient has had just one manic episode and no major depressive episodes.
C) All the client's episodes have been Hypomanic
D) The client may have been misdiagnosed as an alcoholic.

Answer on Page: 89

Question 117   Section: CLINICAL

What is the difference between Bipolar Disorder I and Bipolar Disorder II?

A) Bipolar Disorder I has no depressive episodes
B) Bipolar Disorder II has no depressive episodes
C) Both have very similar symptoms, but type II does not have any "High" phases which lead to hospitalization
D) Both have very similar symptoms, but type I does not have any "High" phases which lead to hospitalization

Answer on Page: 90

Question 118   Section: CLINICAL

A client is referred to you by his family. After an intensive interview with several members of the family you are able to document the following data; 1) For the past 5 days your client has exhibited a mood that is vastly more expansive and elevated than his usual mood. 2) This mood has been sustained for the past 5 days with no reduction, 3) During the past 5 days, they have shown a reduced need for sleep, racing thoughts and grandiosity. 4) There are no signs of psychosis 5) every family member has observed the same behavior. The current episode does not require hospitalization. Your BEST diagnosis would be:

A) Hypomanic Episode
B) Mixed Episode
C) Manic Episode
D) Depressive Episode

Answer on Page: 91

Question 119   Section: CLINICAL

You have just reviewed a case brought to you by a younger and less experienced social worker. It is clear that you are dealing with a Mood Disorder. The current diagnosis is Bipolar I Disorder. It is also clear that the diagnosis is incomplete because the most current episode needs to have a specifier attached. You ask several questions of the social worker and you get the following answers. The patient is extremely sensitive to feelings of rejection, they often feel as if there body is "leaden" (so heavy they cannot do anything) and they tend to overeat and are obese. You tell the social worker they need to add WHICH of the following specifiers:

A) With Atypical Features
B) With Melancholic Features
C) With Catatonic Features
D) With Postpartum Onset

Answer on Page: 92

Question 120   Section: CLINICAL

Which of the following disorders can present the clinical social worker with symptoms of Depression and Mania that can look like a Mood Disorder?

A) Vascular Dementia
B) Personality Disorders
C) Bereavement
D) All of the above

Answer on Page: 92

Question 121   Section: CULTURAL

You practice as a culturally competent social worker, which means you honor and respect the differences between cultures. You are assigned a new client that is a member of an ethnic, racial or social group unfamiliar to you. Your best course of action would be to...

A) Ask the client to help educate you on their culture and
      ethnicity
B) actively seek out information and knowledge on the new
      culture.
C) continue therapy without additional training
D) refer the client to someone who is of their own ethnic
      or cultural group.

Answer on Page: 93

Question 122   Section: CULTURAL

You are a culturally competent social worker who has been assigned to see a Guatemalan immigrant. The immigrant has received a notice from the U.S. Immigration and Customs Enforcement Agency (I.C.E.) requiring him to come in for an interview within the next two weeks. Like most Guatemalan's who have fled the country, he is fearful of all authorities. During your second session he tells you that he is afraid he will be deported if he goes to the appointment because he made a false statement on his immigration paperwork. He is concerned that if he is deported, he will be separated from his girlfriend and their 2 year old son, and they will be forced to fend for themselves. Your primary task to solve this issue is...

A) Convince the client to go the I.C.E. Office and confess the truth.
B) Call I.C.E. yourself and inform them about his status because lying on an immigration application is a crime.
C) Continue to provide services as you have no obligation to report the behavior to I.C.E.
D) Discuss the client's concern and discuss the need for him to get a lawyer and assist him in a referral to a lawyer.

Answer on Page: 95

Question 123   Section: CULTURAL

You are assigned a family and during the assessment, mom and dad tell you that they are seeing you because their son is GAY and they want him changed. The son sits quietly during the exchange and does not respond to any questions other than to shrug and sigh. Mom and dad tell you they want you to refer them to an agency that can provide Reparative or Conversion psychotherapy in order to retrain their son to become a heterosexual. You should respond with...

A) a referral to an agency that practices reparation psychotherapy.

[23]

B) Explain to the parents that there is no shame in being homosexual

C) Let the parents know that NASW, APA and the American Psychiatric Association consider this type of therapy to be UNETHICAL and you will not be able to make a referral.

D) Set up a time to speak with the son alone to see how he feels about Reparation Psychotherapy.

Answer on Page: 96

Question 124   Section: CULTURAL

You have received a case involving an Asian-American youth who is a first-generation immigrant. His parents were born in the far-east and he was born in Texas. As you begin to assess his support system and draw up a treatment plan, you know one of the problems you will face with this client, due to a familiar psychological characteristic, of some Asian cultural groups is ....

A) difficulties in understanding some of the eligibility requirements for psychotherapy

B) an overly exaggerated feeling of shame and possible loss of face due to being "unable" to handle his problems.

C) extreme resistance from his family of origin because they feel "outsiders" should not be involved in their life.

D) None of the above

Answer on Page: 97

Question 125   Section: CULTURAL

You are asked to assess a man from New Guinea regarding a recent behavior he displayed at his work place. He works on the loading docks of a shipping company. The episode was seen by an EAP counselor at the shipping company and they wrote a description of it which included a period of brooding; followed by a violent outburst where he was extremely aggressive towards several dock workers who were taunting him. Immediately after the episode, he began talking about his feelings. He stated he was being persecuted by his fellow workers and then appeared exhausted and quickly returned to his pre-aggressive state. Several minutes later, when questioned about his behavior he appeared to be displaying a significant amount of amnesia. You pinpoint the behavior as...

A)   Amok
B)   Psychotic Disorder
C)   dhat
D)   Hwa-byung

Answer on Page: 98

Question 126   Section: CLINICAL

Bobbi is a 23 year old female who has recently graduated from college and has been unemployed for about 8 months. She is seeking ways to cope with her feelings of depression and guilt. After several sessions, you realize her guilt is related to spending so much on tuition and not having gotten employment. She reports she has very few friends, belongs to no organizations or social clubs and often talks about her most enjoyable times as when she is sitting around home daydreaming. You realize her primary ego defense to cope with this stressor is...

A) Rationalization
B) projection
C) autistic fantasy

D) devaluation

Answer on Page: 99

Question 127   Section: CLINICAL

You begin an assessment on a 36 year old Arab-American, named Saheed. He is self-referred because he feels he is "not-good enough". After extensive questioning, you find it difficult to identify any particular event or person in his life who is negative. When he discusses his family members or his relationships at work, he talks glowingly about people. His entire outlook on life is one of overt optimism. You begin to wonder what brought him to therapy when you realize that his primary ego-defense mechanism is...

A) intellectualization
B) idealization
C) humor
D) isolation

Answer on Page: 100

Question 128   Section: CLINICAL

You have just received a referral on a 22 year old female whose parents are very concerned that she "is unable to stand on her own two feet." They state that she cannot make decisions by herself. After your initial assessment, she is unable to state any specific problems but does tell you that she has several close friends and they always help her when she has problems. When you ask about the type of help they offer, she replies, "They listen and give advice." While you are unable to locate any pathology, you realize she is adept at using the defense mechanism known as....

A) Acting Out
B) Affiliation
C) Altruism
D) Anticipation

Answer on Page: 102

Question 129   Section: CLINICAL

Marcus comes into your clinic with the following self-reported issues. He is convinced that most people dislike him and are upset with him. He states that no matter how hard he tries to start a conversation, he just drives people away. He states that when someone begins to become irritated by him in a conversation he tends to get upset with them, which pushes them away faster. He stated that one of his only friends has often told him that he causes people to dislike himself because of how he behaves towards them, but he is unable to see this side of himself. His friend also tells him he should "repress" his anxiety. You realize he is using the ego-defense mechanism of...

A) Passive Aggression
B) Projective Identification
C) Reaction formation
D) Repression

Answer on Page: 103

Question 130   Section: CLINICAL

Juan and Isobel come to their first couple's session and begin to talk about their issues. Juan is very active in his church and spends a great deal of time traveling to other churches talking about his views on abortion. He is adamantly opposed to Roe V. Wade. He spends so much time spreading his "ministry" that he is hardly ever home and Isobel is tired of being left alone. This has been going on for almost 3 years. Further questioning reveals that about 5 years ago their only daughter went to college and did not come home the first summer. Over winter break of her second year, she revealed to her parents that she had gotten pregnant and had terminated the pregnancy because she did not want to drop out of school. She felt devastated by this and eventually left school to join the Peace Corp. Juan states that he has "come to terms with his daughter's betrayal" and no longer even thinks about it. In fact, he said it has been more than a year since it even crossed his mind. You realize that Juan is using the ego defense mechanism called....

A) Self-observation
B) Self-assertion
C) Sublimation
D) Suppression

Answer on Page: 104

Question 131   Section: CLINICAL

You are working with Mary, a 32 year old divorced mother of three and she has been rather consistent with attending sessions. She often shows up early and never has to be prompted to begin her session. Usually, she brings complaints and problems with her. She complains about her neighbors, her children's teachers, her ex-husband, her new boyfriend and just about everyone involved in her life. When you discuss ways of coping with individual issues she tends to spurn them and when you try to teach or role-play social skills, she seems dismissive. You have assigned several sets of homework and she has not done any of them. When asked about her refusal to do homework, she states, "It won't work anyway, so why waste the time." Your first impression is a person with a personality disorder, however, you also realize Mary is using a specific ego defense mechanism which could mask a personality disorder or cause you to pursue a personality disorder diagnosis when it is not warranted. You know the ego defense mechanism is …

A) Denial
B) Displacement
C) Dissociation
D) Help-rejecting

Answer on Page: 105

Question 132   Section: CLINICAL

You have seen Silvio two times as a referral from the court system. Silvio has been charged with several misdemeanor crimes which do not include battery or violence. You have developed an eco-diagram of his functioning and have noticed he has a very poor relationship with his father, who is not in the home. Silvio does not feel his father is supportive of anything he does. You ask Silvio if he would try a homework task of calling his father and talking to him for two minutes to "just make contact." Silvio's response is quick and harsh, "I know my father hates me, and so there is no point in trying to have a relationship with him!" Because you have worked with adolescents you realize this statement comes directly from a STANDARD THINKING ERROR called…

A) Entitlement
B) Emotional Reasoning
C) Fortune-telling

D) Externalization

Answer on Page:106

Question 133   Section: CLINICAL

You complete an assessment on Tommy, a 14 year-old boy who was brought in by his parents. Tommy's parents say he just sits around and refuses to do anything. When they want to go to a movie, he does not feel like it. When they want to go shopping he would rather stay home. He has no friends and does not appear to be interested in making any.

When you question Tommy about his behavior he seems slightly depressed. When you ask a direct question about his refusal to participate in family life, he responds by saying "it would not be any fun and besides they don't really want me to come anyway." Several more questions return similar answers. Tommy's parents think he may be having a 'nervous breakdown." You have seen similar behavior in adolescents in the past and you believe he actually perceives the world through the lens of a thinking error known as...

A) Image
B) Catastrophizing
C) Jumping to conclusions
D) Mind-Reading

Answer on Page:107

Question 134   Section: CLINICAL

You have taken a job as a prison social worker and one of your first clients of the day is a man serving a life sentence without the possibility of parole. He has served 8 years up to the point where you meet him. When you ask him why he requested an appointment with mental health he begins a long tirade about how everyone is against him. He tells you the dorm sergeant hates him and his fellow dorm members are always causing him problems. You have read his "prison jacket" and realize he has been sentenced for 1st Degree Murder. When you ask about the crime he was sentenced on he tells you it was not his fault. Upon further questioning he decides to tell you his story. He went out one night to rob a local drug dealer because he needed cash. He took his brother's pistol. As he was robbing the dealer, the dealer pulled out a gun and shot him, wounded, but not incapacitated he fired back and killed the drug dealer. He was convinced that since the drug dealer shot him first, he was only acting in self-defense. He then stated that his lawyer "screwed him" because his lawyer refused to use self-defense as a legal defense for his actions. You realize the primary issue facing this inmate/client is his internalization of a specific criminal thinking pattern. You recognize this criminal thinking pattern to be...

A) The "good person" stance
B) the "victim" stance
C) the "lack of time" stance
D) the "unique person" stance

Answer on Page: 108

Question 135   Section: CLINICAL

You have just completed your 4th session with Matthew, a 35 year old male who has served two brief prison terms. The first incarceration was for two years and the second for three. He has been out of prison for 7 years. He identifies himself as a devout church-goer who never misses a service and enjoys being part of his church community. During your sessions he peppers his language with bible quotes and admonitions. He came to therapy for complaints about stress and anxiety in his life. At this beginning of this session he admitted that his stress was caused by a letter he received from the State Police Agency declaring him a "person of interest" in a current investigation involving insurance fraud. He stated that while he is an insurance agent he is also very religious. He does not understand why he is being "targeted" in this investigation. Upon questioning, he admits his prior two incarcerations involve fraud and larceny. He also shows no remorse for his prior actions and seems more upset about getting arrested and losing his job than disappointing his church friends. You realize you may be dealing with a client who has a past diagnosis of anti-social personality disorder and he is deeply involved in the thinking error known as ...

A) fragmented personality
B) justifying
C) fronting
D) grandiosity

Answer on Page: 110

Question 136   Section: ETHICAL

You are a 32 -year-old social worker. You have completed your MSW and are 10 weeks shy of completing your two years of licensure supervision. You have passed the ASWB exam and are simply waiting to finish your last 10 hours of supervision with your clinical supervisor, and then file the paperwork to become fully licensed.

Your agency refers you a case involving a man and woman, who are currently divorced, and are in a dispute over the custody and arrangements for their two children. Your initial meeting is with the husband. During your initial assessment, he lets you know that he feels his ex-wife will be very irate at the fact that they have not been assigned a licensed clinician. He states that his wife is an LCSW. He states she has been licensed for the past 10 years and was adamant in her referral process that she and her ex-husband receive services from a licensed clinical social worker.

It becomes clear to you during your assessment with the ex-husband, that the custody and arrangements for the children, are going to be a very contested issue. You have a number of concerns about the case. You have concerns about the possibility of a clinical intern providing services to a licensed clinical social worker. You decide to call your LCSW clinical supervisor and get feedback on your concerns. After detailing the situation with your supervisor, your supervisor recommends that you do the following actions:

A) continue seeing the divorced couple in therapy.
B) continue seeing the ex-husband in therapy and ask your office to schedule a different commission for the ex-wife.
C) contact the ex-wife and discuss the situation with her and ask if she would be willing to accept you as a clinician.
D) contact your office and explain to them that the case needs to be referred to a licensed provider.

Answer on Page: 111

Question 137   Section: ETHICAL

You are hospital social worker in charge of discharge planning for people in need of inpatient and outpatient rehab. Many of the clients you're responsible for have had traumatic brain injury due to motor vehicle accidents. You have a very firm working knowledge of the different services that Medicaid and Medicare will pay for. You also have good working relationships with most of the rehab centers within a 250 mile radius of your hospital. As part of your job responsibility you often have to interface with the State Department of Health coordinator for brain and spinal cord injury. You have completed your licensure requirements, and are three weeks from being able to file an application to become an LCSW. The state coordinator for the brain and spinal cord injury program is an MSW, approximately your age, who has never signed up as a clinical intern and is not currently seeking licensure. You are meeting with the mother of a 35 -year-old female patient who was severely injured in a motor vehicle accident. You have been trying to find rehab for the client for the past 30 days. The client has been discharged from the hospital 22 days prior however mother refuses to bring her home and no rehab has been willing to except her until today. During your consultation with the mother, the spinal cord injury project coordinator is involved. Multiple times during the conference, the MSW interrupts you and gives the mother inaccurate information regarding the benefits available to her daughter. Several times during the conference, the MSW tells mother that she should demand the hospital pay for certain things, and provide her with certain services before she agrees to take her daughter home.

Your ethical obligation is to respond by:

A) you should ignore the MSW and continue to provide accurate information to mother.
B) you should interrupt the MSW and point out the incorrect information and then continue to try to provide correct information to mother.
C) you should gracefully terminate the conference and reschedule with mother at a time when the social worker is not present.
D) Because you are almost an LCSW you should call down the social worker, point out her errors, and ask her to excuse yourself from the conference.

Answer on Page: 113

Question 138   Section: ETHICAL

You are a clinical social work intern one year post-graduation. You've been providing pro bono counseling services at a local drop-in agency that is a nonprofit. Most of your clients are extremely low income and often have interactions with the department of children family services. You have provided six sessions to a 23 -year-old female client, who is indigent and has a nine month old baby boy. She has a prior mental health history and has been in voluntarily hospitalized three times since age 17. While you have no direct paperwork on her hospitalizations you believe the general diagnosis is psychotic disorder, NOS. You have learned that during her last hospitalization, the nine -month-old child was picked up by the birth father, and is currently living with the birth father and his grandmother. You have no reason to suspect there's any problem with the child living with the birth father and his mother. While you are away from the drop in center you receive a phone call from the secretary saying that "Judy" called you and left a telephone number asking you to call about your client. The secretary told you that the caller identified themselves as someone from the Department of Children and Family Services. You have no verification of any information on Judy, your client has never mentioned this name, and the best of your knowledge the client is not involved Department of Children Family Services. You call your clinical supervisor to staff the case and determine what should be done. Your clinical supervisor recognizes the name of the caller and the phone number from the caller. Your clinical supervisor informed you that the caller is a DCF attorney. Your clinical supervisor then advises you to take the following actions:

A) return the call to Judy and provide her with all information she requires.

B) return the call to Judy and tell her you are unable to give her information without a signed release from your client.

C) asked the secretary to call the call her back and instruct her that all information requests need to come in writing.

D) throw the number away and don't worry about it.

Answer on Page: 115

Question 139   Section: ETHICAL

You have begun seeing a 16 year old female who has health insurance. The insurance has authorized two sessions for assessment but require a diagnosis and treatment plan for further sessions. The parents inform you that they feel their daughter needs services and they do not have the money to pay without the insurance support. Your first session is with the family and your second session is with the girl alone. You have identified the following features: 1) the behavioral or emotional symptoms developed in response to an identifiable event(s) and began within three months of the event (which occurred at school). 2) The behaviors are clinically significant due to responses after exposure to the event that were in excess of what would be expected by someone else, and 3) they cause significant impairment to her schooling because her grades and attendance at school is suffering.

After considering all the facts you have gathered, you decide that she meets the criteria for an Adjustment Disorder with Mixed Emotional Features. Upon reviewing the insurance treatment plan forms, you realize the insurance will not pay for any diagnosis of Adjustment Disorder. You realize that with a little "fudging" of your criteria you could apply a diagnosis of Post-Traumatic Stress Disorder, for which the insurance company would pay. You feel you can help the client and would like to work with them, and you realize the parents are not able to pay you privately. You also do not feel you have the time to provide the services in a pro bono fashion. Your best course of action would be to:

A) Give the diagnosis of Adjustment Disorder and refer the parents to a free clinic where their daughter can see another counselor without the insurance impediment.
B) Give the diagnosis of PTSD and continue to provide services to the girl and receive insurance money for it.
C) Discuss the situation with the parents and ask them if they would be comfortable with you giving the PTSD diagnosis for insurance reimbursement.
D) Provide the services Pro Bono.

Answer on Page: 117

Question 140   **Section: ETHICAL**

You are a hospice social worker, employed by a for-profit hospice. You have a number of clients on your caseload. You have been asked to get a client to sign some paperwork for the office. When reading the paperwork, you realize it is financial in scope. It is paperwork that binds the client to pay for the services provided by the hospice regardless of whether or not the Medicaid, or Medicare will cover the cost. You remember a staff meeting approximately one month ago, where all staff were told that certain clients did not have the Medicaid information entered correctly and therefore Medicaid did not pay for the services. You present the client with the paperwork and explain the purpose of the paperwork. The client states they do not want to sign the paperwork. They stated that upon acceptance to hospice, they were told their Medicaid or Medicare would pay the bill completely. Your best action at this point is:

A) explain to the client that the paperwork must be signed in order for the billing department to have a complete file.

B) tell the client to write the word refused across the signature space and you will turn the paperwork back into the office.

C) tell the client if they do not sign the paperwork you will have to discontinue seeing them and their case may be closed.

D) refuse to present the paperwork to the client and return it to the office unsigned.

Answer on Page: 118

Question 141   Section: CLINICAL

You have been asked to do a family assessment. One member of the family, Michael, is diagnosed with mental retardation. After your assessment you find that Michael can carry out work and self-care tasks with moderate supervision from his family members. You would be able to estimate his FSIQ (Full Scale IQ) as being between:

A) 20-40
B) 50-70
C) 35-55
D) Below 20

Answer on Page: 120

Question 142   Section: CLINICAL

You are working with Jodi and during your second session she states that she is a left handed individual and therefore is more sensitive, more creative and more emotional than many other people who are right handed. You ask her how she knows this and she says, "I just heard it and it fits me." You are aware that she may be correct according to a theory created by Nobel-prize-winners Roger Sperry and Robert Ornstein. This theory is known as...

A) Brain Schism Theory
B) Brain Lateralization Theory
C) Inherent Lobe Theory
D) Corpus Collosum Effect

Answer on Page: 121

Question 143   Section: CLINICAL

You have been seeing Marsha for 3 sessions. Marsha has a rather limited knowledge about medical practices. She stated she recently went to the doctor and he gave her an EEG. She is convinced there is something seriously wrong with her and does not want to go back to the doctor. You understand that an EEG is used to...

A) to provide a graph of the alpha waves of the brain
B) maps the biological conditions inherent in goal-directed behavior.
C) classify mental retardation caused by the presence of an extra chromosome.
D) measure autonomic nervous system functions

Answer on Page: 123

Question 144   Section: CLINICAL

You are seeing Sylvia for anxiety and depression. You have seen her every other week for about 4 months. She is extremely addicted to nicotine, and often has to take a break during your 50 minute session to sneak outside for several puffs on a cigarette. She reports smoking 4 packs a day and is considered a "Chain-smoker". She has just told you she had a positive pregnancy test and is excited about having a baby. She asks if her smoking will have any harmful effects on developing baby. You let her know that the nicotine from the cigarettes could have the following effect on her child...

A) lower than normal birth weight
B) mental retardation
C) flaccid muscle tone
D) Tay Sachs Syndrome

Answer on Page: 123

Question 145   Section: CLINICAL

Michael and Amy have begun seeing you because of problems they report with their two pre-teen age children. When asked to describe how they respond to different parenting situations, it is clear they exhibit a belief in a "hands-off" attitude and letting the children set their own rules. They state this type of attitude will help their children become more internally driven, focused and more self-initiating. They are exhibiting which major style of parenting?

A) Authoritarian
B) Authoritative
C) Uninvolved
D) Permissive

Answer on Page: 125

Question 146   Section: HUMAN DIVERSITY

A 22-year-old homeless woman appears at your community mental health agency. She appears delusional and disorganized. However she states she has eaten daily and knows how to get help. She refuses hospitalization but agrees to maintain phone contact with you.   What is your best response to this situation?

A) Respect her self-determination and ask her what kind of help   she would like.
B) Accompany her to a walk-in psychiatric outpatient emergency   facility.
C) Tell her family to proceed with an involuntary commitment.
D) Determine if other sheltered environments or supports are   available to her.

Answer on Page: 127

Question 147   Section: CLINICAL

Eric Erikson's psychosocial stages of development theory postulate that each stage presents a conflict which the individual must resolve before advancing to the next stage. The stage of the school age child is the fourth stage in his theory and deals with...

A) Industry vs. inferiority
B) Intimacy vs. isolation
C) Integrity vs. despair
D) Identity vs. role confusion

Answer on Page: 127

Question 148   Section: CLINICAL

You are working with an intergenerational family, mom, dad, paternal grandma, maternal aunt and three children. Your treatment plan is to help them create and structure boundaries in order to have a greater sense of control and appropriate behavior. This tactic would be most likely to cause...

A) More family enmeshment
B) Less family enmeshment
C) no change in enmeshment
D) no change in differentiation level

Answer on Page: 130

Question 149   Section: CLINICAL

Pris is a 47 year old white female who is characteristically very shy and withdrawn. She will participate when asked, but will not seek out company. She has decided to enter group treatment and will participate in an "assertiveness training" group. Over the first couple sessions, she experienced lots of self-doubt and uncertainty as to whether this was the "right choice" for her. Her counselor urges her to stay in group because he realizes the mental health process occurring here will subside rather quickly and she will feel better. The mental health process is known as...

A) dissociation
B) acculturation
C) cognitive dissonance
D) individuation

Answer on Page: 131

Question 150   Section: ETHICS

One of the most powerful ethical cases in social work and mental health is the Tarasoff case. The decisions in this case have changed the landscape of how we practice in certain areas. Which of the following areas does the Tarasoff decision NOT AFFECT...

A) Malpractice liability
B) Privileged communication
C) Assessment procedures
D) Confidentiality

Answer on Page: 132

Question 151   Section: CLINICAL

You begin working with a new female client, Dawn, Age 21. Upon reading her history, you learn she has been diagnosed with Borderline Personality Disorder. Which of the following symptoms would the clinician have had to see in order to arrive at this diagnosis?

A) a sustained pattern of excessive emotionality and attention seeking behavior which could be traced back to adolescence.
B) abrupt mood shifts with a poorly developed self-image, and a history of intense and unstable relationships
C) an individual who expects others to perceive them as special or gifted and exhibiting a grandiose and inflated sense of their own worth.
D) an excessive need to be taken care of that leads to submissive and clinging behavior and fears of separation

Answer on Page: 133

Question 152   Section: CLINICAL

You have a social work colleague who is discussing a case with you. He describes several behaviors and the internal as well as social motivation, which drives the client to commit these behaviors. He says he wishes he could understand the ONTOGENESIS of the client. What does he want to know?

A) the various conditions which stimulate an emotional state and/or arousal
B) the overall course of development of an individual
C) the aspects of the behavior which can be used to classify the disorder.
D) the perceptions of the client and their interactions with friends and family.

Answer on Page: 135

Question 153   Section: CLINICAL
You have completed an assessment and initial interview with Jon, a 22-year old male who began having problems 4 months ago. His history is unremarkable before his current symptoms. He presents with an organized delusional system which has an overarching theme of persecution. Your best initial diagnosis would be...

A) Schizoid Personality Disorder
B) Schizophreniform Disorder
C) Paranoid Schizophrenia
D) Schizophrenia, undifferentiated

Answer on Page: 153

Question 154   Section: ETHICS

You are working in a private practice and complete an intake session with the female client, 35 years old. At the end of the assessment she tells you that she is unable to afford the fees for therapy. Her problems appear rather serious, and she appears to be in need of help rather quickly. She also tells you that she is very much interested in receiving help. Your most ethical response, as a social worker is to...

A) tell her that you are sorry that she cannot afford your fee and that she will have to look for services elsewhere.
B) tell her that you believe this is an important set of services for her, given your assessment, and that she should think about approaching her family members in order to borrow money to pay your fees.
C) ask her if she has really explored all the resources around her, and whether or not there was a friend, family member, or a bank that could provide her with the money she needs to pay for your services.
D) tell her you will see what kind of an arrangement you can work out with her, and determine whether or not you can enter into a satisfactory contract with her. Explain to her that if you cannot enter into a contract with her, you will be happy to refer her, and follow up on the linkage, to an agency or another social worker who is able to help her.

Answer on Page: 137

Question 155   Section: CLINICAL

You are a school social worker approached by Maggie, a 17 - year-old female. After several minutes of discussion she confides in you that both she and her 11 -year-old sister has been the ongoing victims of sexual abuse by her stepfather.

She relates to you that her stepfather is an alcoholic, and has been unemployed for the past three years. She states she wishes she had told her mother about the abuse, but she was afraid of what her stepfather would do if she told her mother. She stated the reason she has come forward now is because her stepfather promised not to abuse her 11-year-old sister if she kept "the secret." When she discovered her 11 -year-old sister was being abused, she decided that she could no longer keep "the secret." If this problem were left unreported, which of the following a long-term outcomes might be expected of both the 17 -year-old and in the 11 -year-old abuse victim.

A) you would expect both girls to develop sexual dysfunction in their primary relationships.
B) you would expect both girls to develop long-term patterns of alcohol abuse and alcoholism as a coping mechanism.
C) you would expect both of them to get involved in unhealthy and destructive relationships with the possibility of suicidal thoughts, behaviors, or self cutting behavior.
D) You would expect the girls to choose primary partners in their adult relationships, which would replicate the abuse on their children.

Answer on Page: 138

Question 156   Section: CLINICAL

You have begun seeing a 26 year old female, diagnosed with a dysthymic disorder. Of the following symptoms, which one will most likely be prevalent?

A) Vivid olfactory hallucinations that have begun in the last three   months and have occurred daily.
B) Long-term chronic depression which lasts for most days for approximately 2 years.

C) Drug dependency and drug abuse centered specifically on methamphetamine and stimulants.
D) an inability to maintain a job for any length of time due to intrusive thoughts and flashbacks.

Answer on Page: 139

Question 157   Section: CLINICAL

During a monthly staff meeting your supervisor asks every social work clinician to explain the difference between post-traumatic stress disorder and acute stress disorder as described in the DSM-IV TR. Your best response is

A) The duration of the intrusive thoughts and flashbacks occur for more than one month and can be debilitating.
B) the length of time between the trauma and the onset of the symptoms experienced by the client.
C) The level of somatization which can be observed in the responses to stressors or situations.
D) the degree of trauma, including the nature of the trauma and any pathology that results from it.

Answer on Page: 140

Question 158   Section: CLINICAL

You have been seeing Paul, a 33 year old married male, weekly for 3 months. He initially presented with moderate to severe depression. During your first 3 sessions you convinced him to seek a psychiatric evaluation for possible medication, and he was placed on Luvox, an SSRI (Selective Serotonin Reuptake Inhibitor). Within 4 weeks of his taking the medications you saw his symptoms of irritability, hopelessness and lack of energy virtually disappear. He also related an increase in his overall energy level. Over the last two weeks you have noticed the re-occurrence of his irritability and hopelessness. After several avoided questions, he admits he stopped taking the medication about 2 weeks ago. He states he had problems with it but will not discuss specific issues with you. You should be aware that one of the potential side effects of an SSRI with male clients is...

A) SSRIs can cause symptoms similar to neuroleptic malignant syndrome.
B) SSRIs are almost never covered by health insurance because they are considered experimental in nature.
C) While SSRIs reduce symptoms of depression, they make it all but impossible to feel happiness.
D) SSRIs can cause a loss of sex drive in males and can cause sexual dysfunction, in the form of "lack of erection" and problems "with ejaculation".

Answer on Page: 141

Question 159   Section: Ethical

You are supervising an intake worker at a local mental health clinic. She calls you at 11:15 AM to tell you that a father has just brought his 17 year old daughter into the intake area and she is actively suicidal. You inform the intake worker that she needs to take the client to the psychiatric emergency unit immediately for evaluation and report back afterwards. The intake worker takes the client to the emergency center but they are unable to see her and state it will be about 4 hours before they can evaluate her. The worker is unable to stay away from intake that long and makes an appointment for evaluation the following morning. She sends the client home with her father instructing them to come back in the morning and for the father to keep an eye on his daughter. She does not call you back and inform you of her actions. You do not follow up with her and confirm her actions. During the night, the daughter manages to kill herself. The father sues the agency for malpractice. Which statement best described the liability of the professionals involved?

A) The supervisor bears primary responsibility
B) The intake worker bears primary responsibility
C) The Agency bears primary responsibility
D) The Agency, the intake worker and the professional all bear equal responsibility.

Answer on Page: 141

Question 160   Section: Ethical

In becoming a professional social worker, one marries the NASW Code of Ethics. One of your ethical commitments that is implicit in the NASW Code of Ethics is ...

A) Your obligation to the client trumps your obligation to your employer.
B) Your representation of your client trumps your obligation over society as a whole.
C) Your representation of your client is subordinate to your obligation over other aggrieved individuals.
D) mobilization of clients is secondary to social work advocacy.

Answer on Page: 142

Question 161   Section: Clinical

You have been seeing a patient with depression for several weeks. The patient has not made any direct statements about suicide. They are beginning to show some signs of recovery from their depressive symptoms. Your level of concern about their potential to commit suicide should...

A) Increase
B) Decrease
C) Remain the same
D) Decrease if the client is medicated with an SSRI

Answer on Page: 143

Question 162   Section: Clinical

You are working with a male patient, age 48, who is diagnosed with a Bipolar Disorder. While no direct statements are made, the client shows various signs that would suggest they are contemplating suicide. Your best intervention is to...

A) complete a family genogram and an eco-map in order to determine familial history and support systems.
B) Complete collateral interviews with spouse and possible adult children to determine the extent of the effect of the bipolar disorder.
C) Avoid discussing suicide because people who are not actively contemplating it will be more likely to think about it if you, as the therapist, discuss it.
D) Address your concerns honestly and frankly. Begin a dialogue regarding suicide and your concerns and feelings aboutthe "signs" they are showing.

Answer on Page: 144

Question 163   Section: Clinical-Diagnostic

You have been asked to evaluate a 43 year old female with a long history of chronic alcoholism. You get some history from the family member who brought her to the appointment. She has been battling alcoholism since age 16 and has had long periods of time when she was homeless and her whereabouts were unknown. She presents with short-term memory loss. She compensates for this loss by confabulating (a natural process where she invents memories in order to fill in the blanks caused by the memory loss) and also displays anosognosia (a marked lack of insight or awareness of her current condition). She appears apathetic, confused and often disoriented. The most likely diagnosis is...

A) Korsakoff's syndrome
B) Tardive dyskinesia
C) psychogenic amnesia
D) Alzheimer's disease

Answer on Page: 145

Question 164   Section: Clinical

You have received a referral to work with a male client with schizophrenia. The referral reports problems with reality testing and medication compliance. Which or the following strategies should you NOT worry about when dealing with this client.

A) maintaining present levels of functioning
B) resolving internal psychological conflicts.
C) reorienting patients to present reality.
D) modifying adaptive behavior

Answer on Page: 147

Question 165   Section: Clinical

You are seeing a 23 year old female client who appears rather manipulative. She lives at home with her mother and father and does not work or attend school. She makes the following statement during your second session, "If you really cared about me like my mother cares, you would not charge me for treatment." The client has just performed a ....

A) Displacement reaction
B) counter-transference reaction
C) transference reaction.
D) sublimation experience.

Answer on Page: 148

Question 166   Section: Clinical

You are working with a mother and father who have an 8 year old male child. During the first family session you notice the child does not seem very expressive. Each time the child begins to express emotions the parents jump in and squash it. Twice while describing an incident at school the child becomes emotional and then parents tell him "get control of yourself" and "boys don't whine." With this type of parenting you would expect to see which of the following symptoms currently?

A) high anxiety levels.
B) eating disorders.
C) psychomotor problems.
D) acting-out behavior and somatization

Answer on Page: 149

Question 167   Section: Clinical

You have received a referral for Mr. Candor, a mid-forties married white male with an alcoholic wife who has just been hospitalized after an 11 day drinking binge where she had at least one blackout. In order to cope with his wife's problem drinking, he has read several popular books on the subject and consulted with his medical doctor who is NOT a substance abuse specialist. He also has acquired a book on abnormal psychology and reads it avidly. He admits when his wife is sober, he reads portions of the book that deal with personality disorders and eccentricity out loud to her. He is concerned that his wife is trying to get him to "rescue her" and is being "dependent." Your initial steps in therapy would involve...

A) Support his approach as a clear way to understand his wife
B) explore his feelings about his wife and her possible "dependency on him"
C) Assume his behavior is a defense mechanism which will pass as soon as he accepts his wife's illness
D) work with him to understand his approach is overly intellectual and probably will bear little fruit.

Answer on Page: 150

Question 168   Section: Clinical

As a generalization regarding clients who suffer from drug or alcohol addiction, which of the following statements regarding POOR TREATMENT PROGNOSIS is the MOST accurate?

A) When they suffer from a concurrent anxiety disorder
B) When they are homeless or unemployed
C) When they are over 50 years old
D) When they are also diagnosed with a Borderline Personality Disorder

Answer on Page: 151

Question 169   **Section: Clinical**

Substance Abuse programs that use cognitive behavioral treatment programs have as their major goal...

A) reducing the need for illegal drugs.
B) changing the cognitive and behavioral processes that lead to drug use
C) altering the drug-abusers' emotional need for mood altering drugs
D) offering alternative and less dangerous medications in place of illegal substances

Answer on Page: 152

Question 170   **Section: Clinical**

Of the four common groups of medications taken by the population generally seen in a mental health center, the Selective Serotonin Reuptake Inhibitors (SSRI), The Tricyclic Antidepressants (TCA.s), The monoamine oxidase inhibitors (MAOI's) and the Atypical Antipsychotics . Which of these drugs have the greatest chance of being lethal in a drug overdose?

A) SSRI's
B) MAOI's
C) TCA's
D) Atypicals

Answer on Page: 153

Question 171   **Section: Psychotherapy**

You have just accepted an intake for a court ordered client. When you work with court-ordered clients, often the most difficult issue you will address during the early phases of treatment will be:

A) Your feelings about the crime that brought the client into your office
B) Your client's attempts at manipulation
C) The lack of help available to your client in his community
D) The anger your client feels towards being ordered into treatment.

Answer on Page: 154

Question 172   **Section: Ethics**

You are working with a client in a hospital setting. They indicate that want to run down to the cafeteria and get themselves a cup of coffee and asks you if they can get you a cup of coffee as well. The BEST thing to do is to...

A) Decline the coffee but thank the client for their thoughtfulness.
B) Accept the offer because it is "just a cup of coffee" and it is a token gesture of respect.
C) Decline the offer but offer to walk down to the cafeteria with the client and get your own cup of coffee.
D) Accept their invitation but offer to pay for your coffee.

Answer on Page: 155

Question 173   **Section: Ethics**

You have been seeing a client and started the relationship with a standard informed consent document. There are very few times in the relationship when you can break confidentiality and disclose confidential information about the client without obtaining the informed consent of the client. The BEST answer is...

A) the client's lawyer
B) the client's spouse
C) a law enforcement authority
D) your spouse

Answer on Page: 156

Question 174   **Section: Ethics**

You were seeing a client up until 6 months ago and therapy was successfully terminated. You run into the client and learn they are a gardener and you need gardening work done at your house. You decide to hire them as a gardener. Which of the following BEST describes the situation?

A) You may hire the ex-client as long as you have a clearly written contract explaining duties and expectations.
B) You may hire the client as long as you do not feel the relationship is exploitive.
C) The relationship will be considered a dual relationship but may be acceptable as long as personal issues are not discussed.
D) The relation is considered a dual relationship and is therefore not acceptable under the social worker code of ethics.

Answer on Page: 157

Question 175   **Section: Psychotherapy**

You have received a referral from intake for a family referred for family therapy. After reviewing the file, you focus on one specific "constellation of facts" discovered during the intake. Because of this specific "constellation" of information you decide the family is not appropriate for family therapy and you refer them back for individual sessions. Which is the BEST answer to justify your decision that family therapy would be ineffective with these clients?

A) interpersonal boundaries are routinely violated.
B) family dynamics indicate that members are deceitful and deliberately destructive.
C) the family has an overt pattern of secret-keeping.
D) two of the family members have no desire of intent to cooperate with therapy.

Answer on Page:158

Question 176   **Section: Psychotherapy**

Incest and family dynamics have several commonalities. You are evaluating a family who has been referred for possible incest issues. After the evaluation, you have identified several interaction styles and familial roles which cause you concern. Which of the following family characteristics, would be the BEST indicator incest occurring:

A) serious enmeshment in family relationships with highly stylized roles.
B) attitudes of permissiveness regarding sexuality.
C) permeable boundaries and extreme chaos.
D) Relationships that are high in conflict.

Answer on Page: 160

Question 177   **Section: Psychotherapy**

You have been asked to evaluate a 50 year old female who has spent the last twenty years as a top performer in an advertising firm. Her income was in the six-figures range and she ran an entire department of junior executives. Five month ago, she was released from her contract when the advertising agency was bought out by an international firm. She was told she was no longer in touch with the current market. Multiple networking contacts have left her with no leads. She relates that during the last three months her drinking, which she never considered a problem, has become an issue. She states she spends entire days in her pajamas and sometimes will not leave the house for three or four days in a row. She states she has begun to drink heavily. She stated that in the past two months she has begun hearing voices which tell her she is worthless and stupid. She stated she has never heard these before but she has discovered that drinking more makes the voices go away. The BEST diagnosis for the client is ...

A) 311 Depressive Disorder NOS
B) 296.22 Major Depressive Disorder, Single Episode
C) 296.24 Major Depressive Disorder with Psychotic Features
D) 291.8 Alcohol Induced Mood Disorder

Answer on Page: 161

Question 178   **Section: Psychotherapy**

Children reared in family environments in which parents or other family members abuse or are dependent on alcohol or other substances are likely to be at higher risk for

A) serious physical mobility problems.

B) schizophrenia and bipolar disorders

C) social anxiety and panic attacks

D) neglect, physical or sexual abuse and behavioral problems.

Answer on Page: 164

Question 179   Section: Psychotherapy

You are seeing John, a 20 year old client diagnosed with an anxiety disorder and an alcohol use disorder. Because the anxiety is a mental health issue and the alcohol use is a substance abuse issue, this client is said to have a...

A) Primary Axis II Diagnosis

B) Dual Diagnosis

C) Multi-axial Diagnosis

D) non-axial Diagnosis

Answer on Page: 165

Question 180   Section: Diagnosis and Assessment.

You have been asked to assess a five-year-old child. You have decided to administer the "Draw-a-Person" test in order to help understand a specific dimension of the child's functioning. The BEST reason to administer the test is to determine...

A) Child's gross and fine motor functioning

B) Basic Personality structures

C) Abnormal or pathological thought structures

D) Level of cognitive development/self-image.

Answer on Page: 165

Question 181   **Section: Psychotherapy**

You are a supervisor at a crisis counseling center. One of your social workers approaches you and reports the following symptoms. She states she is frustrated, overwhelmed and feels like she is drowning in the endless stream of complaints she has to field from her clients. She feels she has almost no energy and cannot cope with the different clients on her caseload. You recognize the social worker is suffering classic symptoms of...

A) Counter-transference
B) Depression
C) Projection
D) Stress/Compassion fatigue

Answer on Page: 167

Question 182   **Section: Psychotherapy**

There are many different theories for intervention with a variety of clients. Each different theory focuses on listening to a different aspect of a client's life story. If a therapist listens attentively to understand the issues involved in their client's life currently and does not focus on how the issues of gender and race play into the client's story, It is MOST likely the therapist is using a/an _____ approach.

A) Rogerian person-centered
B) The cognitive behavioral
C) psychodynamic
D) multicultural

Answer on Page: 168

Question 183   **Section: Behavior**

You have been engaged in a supervision session with a less experienced social worker. He asks the following question. Of the four following childhood behaviors, which is more common among boys than girls, you know the BEST answer is...

A) Acting out sexually
B) Aggression
C) Running away
D) Wetting the bed (Enuresis)

Answer on Page: 170

Question 184   **Section: Behavior**

You have been assigned a client who has been diagnosed with a conduct disorder 312.XX. You know this disorder is characterized by the following behavioral set:
A repetitive and persistent pattern of behavior in which the basic rights of others or major age-appropriate societal norms or rules are violated. The disturbance in behavior causes clinically significant impairment in social, academic, or occupational functioning:
Of the following specific behaviors, the client must display three of more within the past 12 months and at least one in the past 6 months. (1) often bullies, threatens, or intimidates others (2) often initiates physical fights (3) has used a weapon that can cause serious physical harm to others (e.g., a bat, brick, broken bottle, knife, gun) (4) has been physically cruel to people (5) has been physically cruel to animals (6) has stolen while confronting a victim (e.g., mugging, purse snatching, extortion, armed robbery) (7) has forced someone into sexual activity (8) has deliberately engaged in fire setting with the intention of

causing serious damage (9) has deliberately destroyed others' property (other than by fire setting) (10) has broken into someone else's house, building, or car (11) often lies to obtain goods or favors or to avoid obligations (i.e., "cons" others) (12) has stolen items of nontrivial value without confronting a victim (e.g., shoplifting, but without breaking and entering; forgery) (13) often stays out at night despite parental prohibitions, beginning before age 13 years (14) has run away from home overnight at least twice while living in parental or parental surrogate home (or once without returning for a lengthy period) (15) is often truant from school, beginning before age 13 years.

According to Sigmund Freud and psychoanalytic theory, the client MOST LIKELY lacks which of the following structures...

A) Ego functioning
B) Structured family system
C) Superego functioning
D) An Authoritative Figure

Answer on Page: 170

Question 185   **Section: Diagnosis**

You have just received a referral for assessment. The mother has just brought her eight year old boy into your office. She is stating that two days ago she found her eight -year-old son in a walk-in closet with a neighborhood child. The door to the walking closet was closed and both children were naked. She has no other information she can give you. She is extremely worried. Your BEST response would be to...

A) Assess the child for oppositional defiant disorder
B) Assess the child for a conduct disorder.
C) Assess the child for attention deficit hyperactivity disorder.

D) Assess the child for possible sexual abuse victimization.

Answer on Page: 171

Question 186   **Section: Psychotherapy**

You are completing the first session with a women recently separated from her significant other after 7 years of co-habitation which she was hoping would culminate in marriage. She has been separated for 6 weeks and she has met "the man of her dreams." She can't stop thinking about him or talking about him to her friends. You realize she is using a common ego defense mechanism. The ego defense mechanism BEST describing her situation is ...

A) Distortion
B) Projection
C) Displacement
D) Intellectualization

Answer on Page: 172

Question 187   **Section: Psychotherapy**

With the publication of his work, Gestalt Therapy Verbatim, Fritz Perls, MD became the most visible and leading proponent of Gestalt Therapy. This therapeutic system views a patient with unexpressed guilt as...

A) Dysfunctional
B) Normal
C) Neurotic
D) Having unfinished business

Answer on Page: 173

Question 188   **Section: Psychotherapy**

You are assessing a 21 year old male client whose father is in prison with a release date 10 years from now. The client's mother was killed in a single car accident and he believes she committed suicide. You have no other information in the crash. He has been raised by his father's sister and her husband. He has not completed high school due to excessive absences and has failed the GED twice. You have received the referral due to variety of issues with both teachers and other students in his GED classes. His reported problems include a pattern of deceitful behavior (which was verified by his aunt) which included repeated 1) lying and attempts to dupe others into activities or behaviors for his personal profit, 2) a failure to plan ahead, 3) an instance where he threw a rock through the window of a garage adjacent to school property and an 4) overall lack of remorse regarding his various behaviors which negatively affect and impact others in his life and 5) the use of aliases in order to steal mail order products. The BEST possible diagnosis would be

A) Conduct Disorder
B) Oppositional Defiant Disorder
C) Narcissistic Personality Disorder
D) Antisocial Personality Disorder

Answer on Page: 175

Question 189   **Section: Psychotherapy**

** A cognitive bias is a pattern of "deviation in judgment" often brought out by a particular situation. It is very easy to allow a cognitive bias to affect your perception.

In the following, you have just received a case and are reading the client's previous file. You realize they have had three admissions during the past two years. In two of the admissions they were diagnosed with Bipolar Disorder NOS and in the third, a Major Depressive Disorder. You decide that they are coming into see you for issues relating to their bipolar diagnosis in order to keep them from needing a re-hospitalization. It is very possible, with that decision, that you have just committed a cognitive bias which will interfere with what you can do to assist them. The BEST description of the cognitive bias you may have used is...

A) Anchoring bias
B) Attentional Bias
C) Bandwagon Bias
D) Bias blind spot

Answer on Page: 179

Question 190   **Section: Psychotherapy**

** A cognitive bias is a pattern of "deviation in judgment" often brought out by a particular situation. It is very easy to allow a cognitive bias to affect your perception.

In the following, you have started an admission on a 38 year old female client who was referred to you because of problems in her marriage. She has stated that she has "caught" her husband in 3 extra-marital affairs over the past 18 years and she thinks there are more. She relates that she is often harshly critical of him and that he has recently "moved onto the couch of a male co-worker" because he does not want to come home anymore. When discussing issues related to separation and possible divorce, she becomes adamant that they will "work things out" and the marriage is strong and will continue. She is utilizing a cognitive bias to cope with her fear of future actions. The BEST description of the cognitive bias she is using is...

A) Negativity bias
B) Neglect of probability
C) Normalcy bias
D) Omission bias

Answer on Page: 180

Question 191   **Section: Diagnosis**

The DSM IV TR lists a series of diagnoses which can only be used with children under the age of 18 or which can be given to a child prior to the age of 18. Of the following disorders, which CAN NOT be applied during childhood (Less than 18 years of age)?

A) 299.10 Childhood Disintegrative Disorder
B) 299.00 Autistic Disorder
C) 307.3 Stereotypic Movement Disorder
D) 301.7 Antisocial Personality Disorder

Answer on Page: 180

Question 192   **Section: Diagnosis**

You know the Diagnostic and Statistical Manual uses a Multi-axial system for diagnosis. Axis I is for issues of Major Clinical concern, and Axis II are for personality disorders and mental retardation. Using this system, what information is coded on Axis V...

A) Social Functioning and Assessment

B) Provisional Diagnoses
C) Global Assessment of Functioning
D) None of the Above

Answer on Page: 185

Question 193   Section: Diagnosis

Psychoanalytic theory postulates there are three major functioning portions of the personality (consciousness). Each portion has specific duties and acts within specific arenas to help the client function productively. The personality portion which assists the individual in working through the consequences of their behavior and helps them weigh outcome measures and costs is known as the ...

A) EGO
B) SUPEREGO
C) ID
D) LIBIDO

Answer on Page: 187

Question 194   Section: Diagnosis

The Diagnostic and Statistical Manual of Mental Disorders (DSM) is used in the United States. All other countries use the International Classification of Diseases Volume 10 (ICD-10). The primary purpose of the DSM in our work as clinical social workers is in...

A) locating the best approach to treatment
B) mapping the etiology of a disorder
C) evaluating a prior diagnosis.
D) Assessing the client

Answer on Page: 190

Question 195   **Section: Diagnosis**

You are working with a client who has a full scale IQ (FSIQ) of approximately 40. Your BEST diagnosis on Axis II would be that of...

A) Borderline Intellectual Functioning
B) Autism
C) Mild Mental Retardation
D) Moderate Mental Retardation

Answer on Page: 190

Question 196   **Section: Diagnosis**

You have begun working with a child who has been diagnosed with a conduct disorder. You interpret the world according to Freudian psychoanalytic principles. According to Freud's principles, this child is manifesting a conduct disorder because they **MOST LIKELY** lack;

A) Ego functioning
B) Superego functioning
C) An Authoritarian parent
D) a rigid family structure

Answer on Page: 191

Question 197   **Section: Diagnosis**
You have a referral on a child who is described as "latency aged". Without looking at the chart, you know the child is between the ages of...

A) Birth to 1 year
B) 1-3 years old.
C) 6-12 years old.
D) 3-6 years old.

Answer on Page: 192

Question 198   **Section: Ethics**

You have been seeing a client for 11 sessions and have been addressing issues including anger, aggression, and impulse control particularly regarding the relationships of people close to him. During a session where you are providing him with psychoeducation concerning aggression as a behavior which is under his voluntary control, he becomes hostile, gets up and leaves. About 4 weeks later you receive a letter from him stating he has started seeing another therapist and you need to release his entire record to him immediately, so he can give it to his new social worker. You believe there is the possibility of serious harm if the record is released to him. You contact him and explain you can release a case summary to the new therapist; however, you cannot release the file to him. He threatens legal action if he does not get the file immediately. In order to keep from committing an ethical violation, you should do which of the following FIRST?

A) Contact an attorney
B) Document the request by the patient and include the reason for non-release
C) Refuse to release the information.
D) Document your concerns about release and then provide the   records to the client.

Answer on Page: 193

Question 199 Section: Diagnosis

As an emergency room social worker, you are asked to evaluate an emergency admission. The client is a 46 year old African-American retired soldier who has served three tours in the Middle East in combat. His wife is reporting she called police because her husband and she were watching a television show when a commercial showed a series of explosions. He became very agitated, began shaking uncontrollably and crawled behind his chair and refused to come out. Your MOST LIKELY diagnosis would be...

A) Psychotic Break
B) Acute Panic Attack
C) Adjustment Disorder with mixed emotional features
D) Post Traumatic Stress Disorder

Answer on Page: 194

Question 200 Section: Assessment

You HAVE been asked to assess a Hispanic client. During the initial portion of the interview, you realize they are not very proficient in English. You begin to explain confidentiality for informed consent and the client appears to be getting upset and seems very frustrated. Your next BEST action would be to ...

A) Give the client your agency's written policy on client confidentiality
B) Ask them why that are getting angry and frustrated
C) Ask the client to tell you, in their own words, what they heard you say and want they understood.

D) Refer the client to a social worker who is fluent in Spanish.

Answer on Page:198

ANSWERS

Question 101   Section: Psychotherapy

The correct answer is C

Part of the mandate of social work is to meet a client "where they are at." In this case the clients are in crisis. As all parents do, these parents have goals and aspirations for their children and have probably plotted out a "life-story" for their child, including the 'son-in-law' and the 'grandchildren'. This life script is about to be shattered. On some level they are wondering how they are going to be able to share a Thanksgiving dinner in the future with their daughter and her 'wife'. Help them through their despair and disappointment and then provide them access to a support group. They need to build a new future story for their family, and interacting with other parents who have done this task will ultimately be very helpful.

A is INCORRECT

Conversion therapy, sometimes called reparative therapy or reorientation therapy, is one type of sexual orientation change effort that attempts to change the sexual orientation of a person from homosexual or bisexual to heterosexual. These types of therapies have been a source of intense controversy in the United States and other countries. The American Psychiatric Association states that political and moral debates over the integration of gays and lesbians into the mainstream of American society have obscured scientific data about changing sexual orientation "by calling into question the motives and even the character of individuals on both sides of the issue." The most high-profile contemporary advocates of conversion therapy tend to be conservative Christian groups and other religious organizations. The main organization advocating secular forms of conversion therapy is the National Association for Research & Therapy of Homosexuality (NARTH), however, NARTH often partners with religious groups.

The American Psychological Association defines conversion therapy as therapy aimed at changing sexual orientation. The American Psychiatric Association states that conversion therapy is a type of psychiatric treatment "based upon the assumption that homosexuality per se is a mental disorder or based upon the a priori assumption that a patient should change his/her sexual homosexual orientation." Psychologist Douglas Haldeman writes that conversion therapy comprises efforts by mental health professionals and pastoral care providers to convert lesbians and gay men to heterosexuality by techniques including aversive treatments, such as "the application of electric shock to the hands and/or genitals," and "nausea-inducing drugs...administered simultaneously with the presentation of homoerotic stimuli," masturbatory reconditioning, visualization, social skills training, psychoanalytic therapy, and spiritual interventions, such as "prayer and group support and pressure."

Mainstream American medical and scientific organizations have expressed concern over conversion therapy and consider it potentially harmful. The advancement of conversion therapy may cause social harm by disseminating inaccurate views about sexual orientation. The ethics guidelines of major mental health organizations in the United States vary from cautionary statements to recommendations that ethical practitioners refrain from practicing conversion therapy (American Psychiatric Association) or from referring patients to those who do (American Counseling Association).

Reference: http://en.wikipedia.org/wiki/Conversion_therapy

B is INCORRECT
Nowhere in the vignette does it state that the girl has problems with her orientation. It appears that she is comfortable and assured. The problem here is with the feelings, aspiration and views of the family.

D is INCORRECT
While every client could ultimately benefit by education, in this situation the primary focus needs to be on alleviating the fear and anxiety caused by their daughter's revelation.

Question 102   **Section: Psychotherapy**

The correct answer is D
Pica is a condition we know little about. Symptoms must occur for at least one month. There is no clear treatment or prognosis. Sometimes Pica lasts for several months and then stops on its own and other times it persists for a lifetime.

Further information:
Pica is a pattern of eating non-food materials (such as dirt or paper).

Causes, incidence, and risk factors
Pica is seen more in young children than adults. Between 10 and 32% of children ages 1 - 6 have these behaviors.

Pica can occur during pregnancy. In some cases, conditions due to a lack of certain nutrients, such as iron deficiency anemia and zinc deficiency, may trigger the unusual cravings. Pica may also occur in adults who crave a certain texture in their mouth.

Symptoms
Children and adults with pica may eat:
Animal feces – Clay – Dirt – Hairballs – Ice – Paint – Sand

This pattern of eating should last at least 1 month to fit the diagnosis of pica.

Signs and tests
There is no single test that confirms pica. However, because pica can occur in people who have lower than normal nutrient levels and poor nutrition (malnutrition), the health care provider should test blood levels of iron and zinc.

Blood tests can also be done to test for anemia. Lead levels should always be checked in children who may have eaten paint or objects covered in lead-paint dust to screen for lead poisoning.

The health care provider should test for infection if the person has been eating contaminated soil or animal waste.

Treatment
Treatment should first address any missing nutrients or other medical problems, such as lead exposure. Treatment involves behavioral, environmental, and family educational approaches. Other successful treatments include associating the pica behavior with bad consequences or punishment (mild aversion therapy) followed by positive reinforcement for eating the right foods.

Medications may help reduce the abnormal eating behavior, if pica occurs as part of a developmental disorder such as mental retardation.

Expectations (prognosis)
Treatment success varies. In many cases, the disorder lasts several months, then disappears on its own. In some cases, it may continue into the teen years or adulthood, especially when it occurs with developmental disorders.

Complications

- Bezoar *(a mass of indigestible material trapped inside the body, usually in the stomach)*
- Infection
- Intestinal obstruction
- Lead poisoning
- Malnutrition

Prevention
There is no specific prevention. Getting enough nutrition may help.

References
1.   *Boris NW, Dalton R. Vegetative disorders. In: Kliegman RM, Behrman RE, Jenson HB, Stanton BF, eds. Nelson Textbook of Pediatrics. 18th ed. Philadelphia, Pa: Saunders Elsevier; 2007:chap 22.*
2.   *Brittenham GM. Disorders of iron metabolism: Iron deficiency and iron overload. In: Hoffman R, Benz EJ, Shattil SS, et al, eds.Hematology: Basic Principles and Practice. 5th ed. Philadelphia, Pa: Elsevier Churchill Livingstone; 2008:chap 36.*
Review Date: 2/28/2010.

Question 103   **Section: Psychotherapy**

The correct answer is B
Jayne could clearly benefit from individual therapy in order to examine her choices and to become aware of their consequences. She will also need help in coping with the effects her parents' divorce had on her and the current pressure it puts on her. Remember, the yelling began at age 12 and a half, just when she was starting into the Erickson Stage of Identity vs. Role Confusion. Up to that point in time she

perceived her family live as stable, but just as she begins to enter a very difficult stage of development, her family life crumbles and she not only has to wrestle with "How am I different from my parents?" and "who am I?", but she has to do it with the foundation of her world split in two.

The parent also need help to keep themselves from doing even more damage to Jayne. They need to understand that their new situation (divorce) is their "normal" situation and they need help in understanding how to cope with their new situation as well as strategies for healing and rebuilding their lives.

A is INCORRECT
This approach would probably help Jayne in the long run, as her current peer group appears to be Detention Center Bound, but it does nothing to address the needs of the parents or multi-family unit.

C is INCORRECT
Continuing Individual therapy = YES; Telling the Parents is a stage she will grow out of = NO. Our society takes illegal drug use very seriously. A conviction can bar a child from entering college and certain Felony Drug Charges make a person unable to get Federal Financial Aid for college. Also Prior drug arrests will limit the choices of the child in employment and career goals including Military Service in most branches. Drug use can have a devastating effect on a child's future plans.

D is INCORRECT
I am all for using the resources offered by your Church, Synagogue, Mosque, or Temple, however, the standard bias that "these kids behavior better" is unproven, and this answer does not address the needs of the family. Once you achieve progress on other goals, this would be a rather good choice.

Question 104   Section: ETHICS

The correct answer is B
Because it is a first session and you do not know the client, it is important you make safety your first concern. You do not know if they will show up alone or with other people, you do not know there mental state and you do not know if there are other aspects of their live that could harm the counseling relationship. The first aspect of the question touches upon the possibility of rape or sexual violence, however, the question does not address the sex of the client. Even if it was a male social worker and the client were a female, there would be no way to dispute a charge of sexually inappropriate behavior made by the client if no one was there. Another possibility: what if the client was a female and domestic violence survivor and was stalked by her ex-partner. You could get injured or killed in an altercation.

A is INCORRECT
While you may find a sympathetic co-worker, you really need to complete initial assessments in a place and at a time when the entire staff is there. It is the most violate part of the therapeutic process and the time when you know the least about the client.

C is INCORRECT
Always think about your safety. One of the ways you become an experienced and well-seasoned social worker is to remain alive. Death and severe injury generally limit your career.

D is INCORRECT
This is a HIPAA violation and can get you sued, reprimanded, fired and have your license revoked.

Question 105   **Section: ETHICS**

The correct answer is D
{Test Strategy: You must answer the questions with ONLY the information given.} Without a release or specific permission, you can not acknowledge that Margaret is your client, let alone appointment times and other information regarding the sessions. A polite but firm, "I can neither confirm nor deny that the person you are calling about is a client. I am sorry I cannot be of assistance to you." usually does the trick. If they keep asking, keep repeating this phrase until they hang up.

HINT: early in my career I worked on a locked, psychiatric facility that functioned as a multi-county intake for indigent psychiatric clients. We had this simple message types out and posted above the phone. We were instructed to simply repeat the message until the caller 'got the point.' It worked!

A is INCORRECT
You have just breached confidentiality. Now the caller, who may or may not be the husband knows Margaret is receiving mental health services, but also knows when and where she will be. If he is a stalker, or dangerous, you have placed both yourself and your client in danger.

B is INCORRECT
You have just acknowledged Margaret as your client and let 'someone' know she is receiving mental health services.

C is INCORRECT
See the answer for A!

Question 106   **Section: CLINICAL**

The correct answer is C
Alopecia - means loss of hair from the head or body. Think
BALDNESS. While not a psychotic symptoms, men suffering
from this often act in ways that seem psychotic (smile) in order
to keep their hair.

A is INCORRECT
DELUSIONS ARE a symptom of psychosis! They are a false
belief that cannot be explained by the client's culture, education
or past experience.

B is INCORRECT
NEGATIVE SYMPTOMS are a symptom of psychosis! They
include a marked reduction in fluency of speech and a loss of
the will to do things. (Known as AVOLITION)

D is INCORRECT
DISORGANIZED SPEECH is a symptom of psychosis! This
includes speech where the mental associations are governed
by puns, rhymes, and other rules that the listener does not
know. In order to be considered disorganized speech, it must
significantly interfere with communication.

Question 107   **Section: CLINICAL**

The Correct answer is D
Negative symptoms are deficits of normal emotional responses
or of other thought processes, and respond less well to
medication. They commonly include flat or blunted affect and
emotion, poverty of speech (alogia), inability to experience
pleasure (anhedonia), lack of desire to form relationships
(asociality), and lack of motivation (avolition). Research
suggests that negative symptoms contribute more to poor

quality of life, functional disability, and the burden on others than do positive symptoms. People with prominent negative symptoms often have a history of poor adjustment before the onset of illness, and response to medication is often limited.

Ref: http://en.wikipedia.org/wiki/Schizophrenia

A is INCORRECT
It is only one of a number of NEGATIVE SYMPTOMS.

B is INCORRECT
It is only one of a number of NEGATIVE SYMPTOMS.

C is INCORRECT
It is only one of a number of NEGATIVE SYMPTOMS.

Question 108   Section: CLINICAL

The correct answer is D
A bizarre delusion is something that is so far from usual life experiences that if told to most people, they would not understand it and would probably regard the event to have been unlikely to occur.

A is INCORRECT
Disorganized thought can be seen in certain subtypes of schizophrenia. An example would be, "thought blocking". When a person stops abruptly in the middle of a thought, then states the feel the thought has been taken or plucked out of their head, and then start making up unintelligible words.

B is INCORRECT
A False Belief is often bizarre and unusual, however, the power to which one holds onto a false belief is much less than the power to which someone clings to a delusion. A false belief

may be able to be shaken, but a delusion will persist, sometimes even after the client is stabilized on medication.

"ELVIS is ALIVE and living in Newark NJ!" is an example of a false belief.

C is INCORRECT
A Hallucination is a false perception in the absence of any sensory stimulus that is related to the event. If someone is sitting next to you at STARBUCKS and you perceive them as an alien invader, you are DELUSIONAL. If NOONE is sitting next to you at STARBUCKS and you perceive an alien invader there, you are HALLUCINATING.

Question 109   Section: CLINICAL

The correct answer is D
Unless the employment history specifically deals with a precipitating factor of the illness it is probably irrelevant. Now, it is quite possible that an event that occurred in the employment arena was a PRECIPITATING FACTOR, but the employment story as a whole is not a direct factor.

A is INCORRECT
Because duration of symptoms is EXTREMELY IMPORTANT in diagnosing issues. Length of time of current episodes and previous episodes are major markers for diagnosis. If duration of illness is less than six months (in general) it is more likely to be a non-chronic condition, but a duration longer than six months tends to be a indicate more chronic conditions. NOTE: Please DO NOT diagnose someone as schizophrenic with less than six months data or observation. It causes concern and confusion to the therapist that follows you. Be conservative! A Brief Psychotic Reaction or a Reactive Psychosis is more reasonable than schizophrenia.

B is INCORRECT
Precipitating Factors are EXTREMELY IMPORTANT in diagnosis. Emotion distress, severe stress, chronic medical conditions, postpartum depression, and drug use can all look like PSYCHOSIS. Remember, sometimes a brief reactive psychosis is occasionally very function at dealing with serious issues and in allowing the client to "Save themselves" when all other tools fail.

C is INCORRECT
Premorbid Personality is EXTREMELY IMPORTANT to diagnosis. People who are happy, pleasant and optimistic and then experience a psychotic reaction would lead you along a different path of inquiry than someone who is depressed, sad and hostile. It is good to remember that all behavior is functional on some level.

Question 110   Section: CLINICAL

The correct answer is C
Family Illness is not an exclusion for schizophrenia

A is INCORRECT
Symptoms of Psychosis can be mimicked. Abuse of street drugs including cocaine, alcohol, stimulants can cause symptoms of psychosis. Some prescription medicines including adreno-corticosteroids can produce symptoms of psychosis.

B is INCORRECT
Mood disorders can often mimic psychosis or can move a person into a psychotic state. Extreme depression, mania, manic episodes can all cause psychotic-like symptoms.

D is INCORECT

Certain medical conditions can cause PSYCHOSIS. These include hypothyroidism and LUPUS. Always rule out possible medical causes before making a diagnosis.

Question 111   Section: CLINICAL

The correct answer is D

A is INCORRECT (When Chosen ALONE)
We know that schizophrenia has a familial component. It tends to run in families. This may indicate a genetic linkage, but the problem is far too complex, and our knowledge of genetic expression is far too meager to fully understand it. If a close relative (Mother, Father, sister, brother) the risk of schizophrenia increases markedly. A less close relative (Uncle, cousin, nephew, niece) and the risk is higher than normal, but not as elevated as a close relative risk.

B is INCORRECT (When Chosen ALONE)
If a client has a history of positive response to lithium in their past, it is most likely the psychotic state is due to a mood disorder, and not schizophrenia.

C is INCORRECT (When Chosen Alone)
Onset of schizophrenia occurs as early as mid teen and on into the middle 20's. It is rather rare for it to develop later in life. If onset of illness is after age 40, you should be looking at a mood disorder or a delusional disorder. Remember, this is only a guideline, schizophrenia can manifest itself in the later years.

Question 112   Section: CLINICAL

The correct answer is C
Schizophrenia affects about 1% of the adult population. Adequate treatment almost always requires neuroleptic

medications which can have very severe side effects, including Tardive Dyskinesia, and usually must be taken for the rest of a patient's life, or symptoms will return.

A is INCORRECT
5% is too high a figure. The CHRONICITY of Schizophrenia (How chronic it is) tends to be lifelong. Once symptoms starts, it is very likely that the person will continue to have symptoms of the disorder for the rest of their life, which will need to be controlled with medications.

B is INCORRECT
5% is too high a figure. However, the second half of this answer is accurate, symptoms tend to be lifelong. (High CHRONICITY)

D is INCORRECT
While the percentage is correct, the impact on social and work function is usually profound. The disorder is lifelong, usually requires medication, symptoms can re-occur and adjustment can be extremely difficult for the patient.

Question 113   Section: CLINICAL

The correct answer is B
Distractibility and disorientation which causes or contributes to material impairment of work, social interactions, studying, or the ability to provide self-care all fall under the rubric of COGNITIVE DYSFUNCTION.

A is INCORRECT
Often the patient with schizophrenia will not believe they are ill and will refuse to accept medications. This inability to accept their condition and accept the changes that will occur due to their condition often lead to major problems.

C is INCORRECT
Dysphoria is a more global term used to cover anxiety, anger, disgust, depression and any other negative emotional set a client presents with.

D is INCORRECT
All three are symptoms of schizophrenia.

Question 114   Section: CLINICAL

The correct answer is D
Residual Schizophrenia is used to diagnose a person when they have had previous episodes and are currently in a temporary remission. Episodic means they are still prone to full episodes and Interepisode defines the condition of still showing some negative symptoms between episodes.

A is INCORRECT
This set of symptoms defines a Schizophrenic diagnosis that would be described as Catatonic Type. The key points are the catalepsy and marked negative symptoms.

B is INCORRECT
This set of symptoms is too vague to classify and should probably be listed as Schizophrenia, Undifferentiated Type.

C is INCORRECT
This set of symptoms describes Schizophrenia, Disorganized type. The important features being; talk gibberish, neglect their appearance and neglect their hygiene.

Question 115 Section: CLINICAL

The correct answer is D
All of the answers are correct. No particular social class or race is affected more by mood disorders or is shielded from the affects of mood disorders. People without a "significant other", or who are single, widowed, divorced show a higher prevalence of mood disorders. While women have a higher rate of mood disorders than men, the occurrence of mood disorders is increasing throughout the general population.

A is INCORRECT (When chosen alone)
Women do have almost twice the rate of mood disorders as men. We need to remember that the data used by the DSM IV was collected primarily in the United States and may not translate well into other countries. My suspicion is that the difference between men and women in this country is related to the different ways men and women are socialized as well as physiological issues.

B is INCORRECT (when chosen alone)
Social class and race do not appear to have a serious impact on the prevalence of mood disorders.

C is INCORRECT (When chosen alone)
Single individuals seem to have more problems with mood disorders than married couples. This could be due to the stress of living alone or is could be that there is no one to notice the beginning of the mood disorder so the disorder becomes worse before help is sought.

Question 116 Section: CLINICAL

The correct answer is B

The diagnosis of mood disorder is very complicated and requires a tremendous amount of information gathered from family, friends, patient, patient records, past hospitalizations and any other information source you can find. If you are going to diagnose a mood disorder, (and do it properly) you should spend hours collecting data, more hours organizing and sifting through the data, create a chart of all the data and then use the diagnostic trees in the back of the DSM IV-TR.

A is INCORRECT
This would be more accurately described as 296.4 Bipolar Disorder I, Most Recent Episode Manic

C is INCORRECT
A person who presented with hypomanic episodes would probably not be diagnoses as a Bipolar Disorder. They may have a mood disorder of unspecified type or you may not have enough information to make a diagnosis.

D is INCORRECT
Probably not! Alcoholism is diagnosed in as many as 30% of Mood Disorders. It is often assumed that alcoholics are self-medicating bipolar disorders. This may be common wisdom, but do not let it lead you away from the data. If you do not have enough information, you need to gather more data.

Question 117   Section: CLINICAL

The correct answer is C
Bipolar I and II are very similar and have almost identical criteria. The distinction between the two deals with the amount of discomfort or disability caused by the "High" phase. In Type II, the High phase never leads to hospitalization and the episodes are more "hypomanic".

A is INCORRECT
Both Types I and Type II have depressive symptoms interspersed among "High" phases.

B is INCORRECT
Both Types I and Type II have depressive symptoms interspersed among "High" phases.

D is INCORRECT
Bipolar Type I is characterized by the overall disability and hurt caused to the client by BOTH the "High" phase and the depressive phase.

Question 118   Section: CLINICAL

The correct answer is A
All six symptoms are classic for a hypomanic episode. The important pieces are: NO psychosis and NO Hospitalization needed. Other symptoms would include if the episode DID NOT markedly interfere with work or social functioning. The final qualifier is the episode is NOT CAUSED by a general medical condition, substance use or reactions to prescription medications.

B is INCORRECT
Mixed Episodes CAUSE psychotic features require hospitalization and markedly impair social, work or personal functioning.

C is INCORRECT
In the Manic Episode the psychotic symptoms are FLORID, which mean they "shine in the night", so to speak. The average person would realize something was wrong even if they did not know them

D is INCORRECT
The criteria for a depressive episode include a period of time of at least 2 weeks where the patient feels depressed (to the point of not being able to enjoy life) and has problems with eating, sleeping, loss of energy, feelings of guilt, trouble concentrating or thoughts about death.

Question 119   Section: CLINICAL

The correct answer is A
All of these features are part of the ATYPICAL Features specifier.

B is INCORRECT
Melancholic Features are specified by symptoms of classic depression. The patient will wake early and feel worse as the day gets later. They lose appetite and weight; they feel guilty and are either agitated or functioning "slowly". When something good happens for them, they do not feel better

C is INCORRECT
Catatonic Features are specified when the client either has excessive motor activity or extreme inactivity. Remember, all catatonic behaviors deal with some type of motor activity.

D is INCORRECT
Postpartum Onset deals with symptoms that occur AFTER the Birth or Miscarriage of a child. (Abortion would be considered a miscarriage for the purpose of this discussion.) The onset of symptoms usually occurs within a month of the incident, but can be delayed.

Question 120   Section: CLINICAL

The correct answer is D

All of these Disorders have depressive and/or manic features that can confuse the clinician who HAS NOT gathered a detailed and extensive history.

A is INCORRECT (When chosen alone)
Vascular Dementia is a Cognitive Disorder. Like Dementia of the Alzheimer's Type, they can be accompanied by delirium, depression, anxiety and extremely altered mood.

B is INCORRECT (When chosen alone)
Of the 10 specific personality disorders, Borderline, Avoidant, Histrionic and Dependent all exhibit signs of altered mood which can be mistaken for other problems if you do not have enough information.

C is INCORRECT (When chosen alone)
Grief and sadness when dealing with the death of a loved one can appear very severe. When evaluating a person who appears to have a mood disorder two or more months after the death of a loved one, it is generally a good idea to find out about the length and depth of the relationship and any other factors surrounding the interactions. People who have been married for 30 or more years should be expected to present with great depression, as do parents who have lost a child.

Question 121   Section: CULTURAL

The correct answer is B
Look at each new client as an opportunity to expand your knowledge and experience. Start with some research on the internet and then try to find other people from the culture and ask questions. Every culture is incredibly complex. Also, when counseling a person with a very different cultural background, do not be afraid to let them know about your lack of knowledge.

As the therapist, you are there to 'guide' the session and allow growth; you are not there to be the omnipotent know-it-all.

A is INCORRECT

The difference between A and B is subtle. Once you start counseling, you can certainly ask the client about aspects of their culture. The portion of counseling that is a combined effort will allow this. But, they are not your social-cultural teacher, they are your client. You need to respect that boundary. The job of learning about their culture falls squarely on your shoulders and not theirs.

C is INCORRECT

Every patient, whether they are from a different culture or not should be a learning experience for you. Indifference in the face of learning will make you a mediocre to bad therapist.

HINT: Once you feel like you know enough, you are probably at your most ignorant and need to redouble your efforts to learn more.

D is INCORRECT

Only do this if there appears to be NO WAY of connecting with and creating a therapeutic bond with a client. There are rare times when someone is from a sufficiently different culture that you will not be able to reach them. However, do not think that being able to work with someone is the same as being able to work well with them. I worked at a practice years ago that had some "Christian Counselors." In many ways their style of counseling was more like that of a clergyman or minister. A client I was referred wanted one of these counselors but there were no appointments so he agreed to see me. After three sessions, I transferred him to a Christian Counselor as the first appointment became available. He was from a specific branch of Protestantism called **"FOURSQUARE"** and his religious belief systems were so ingrained into his life that it was clear he should be helped by someone who could "focus the message" of therapy through the specific lens he needed. Upon reflection, I wasted three of his insurance-allotted twelve sessions.

NOTE: When dealing with people who have been incarcerated in the State or Federal Prison system for any length of time, be especially sensitive to the "prison culture" from which they come. Prison has a very different culture that overrides race, ethnicity and personality. In order to survive (emotionally, mentally or even physically) in you need to adapt to this culture and accept it. It can take years to "throw off" this cultural blanket after a person is released.

Question 122   Section: CULTURAL

The correct answer is D
Think of this situation from the viewpoint of the need for services. Your client's primary need is legal assistance. If he has an immigration problem it is serious and he should have legal representation during his involvement. This situation could have repercussions for his girlfriend and their baby.

A is INCORRECT
You are a clinician, not an attorney. The unauthorized practice of law is a felony. This answer hinges on the word "truth". You do not know what the truth is. What the client believes is a false statement on his application may be nothing, a technicality or something very serious. These are all questions for a lawyer to deal with. You are under no obligation to get him to "turn himself in" because there is no clear indication that a "crime" has been committed.

B is INCORRECT

Once again, you are not an attorney. No crime has been committed that you know of. It would be inappropriate for you to make a judgment on your client's legal status. Immigration is a "hot button" topic and feelings tend to run high around immigration issues. Be sure to keep your cool and not get swept away in the hype.

C is INCORRECT
There is a clearly identified need. You cannot ignore it. You must assist the client in understanding his problem and should make a clear referral. If you do not know a lawyer who deals in immigration law, USE THE PHONE BOOK. Also, other immigration resources include your local Catholic Social Services (it does not matter if your client is Catholic) and in larger metropolitan areas, the local Jewish Social Services Agency, once again, the client does not have to be Jewish to access Jewish Social Services.

Question 123   Section: CULTURAL

The correct answer is B
It is apparent from the interaction that the parents are ashamed and embarrassed by the current situation. Like most people, this is not the "story" they have written for their lives. Their story included a man-women marriage, grandkids and time spent with their son's new family. While grandchildren are possible, the parents cannot see anything currently except their pain and loss at their "story " changing. As a therapist, start with a non-judgmental attitude and proceed with helping the parent accept their new roles. Their disappointment will be directed at their son, however, the root cause of their disappointment is the loss of their "dream" or their projection for the future.

A is INCORRECT

Regardless of your personal belief systems, Reparation therapy is considered by all National counseling Agencies as UNETHICAL TREATMENT and could result in the loss of your license. Regardless of your belief system, the client always has the right to direct the course of therapy. If your viewpoints get in the way, you may need to make a referral to another counselor.

C is INCORRECT
This is a clear statement of FACT.

D is INCORRECT
You should choose this option ONLY if you are planning the leave the field as a licensed therapist. It would be a great way to end your career.

Question 124   Section: CULTURAL

The correct answer is C
It is a standard fixture of Asian Culture that outsiders should not be involved. There is a very long standing streak of Xenophobia in some Asian cultures. Regardless of how your client feels about his problems, his family is likely to feel shame and embarrassment at his "going to an outsider" to seek help. Asian culture also puts a very high priority on "Handling Your Own Problems" and "Bear your own problems without complaining". These are all issues that you need to keep in your consciousness when working with a 1st or 2nd generation Asian American.

A is INCORRECT
Almost no one has problems understanding the eligibility requirements for psychotherapy. The only eligibility

requirement I am aware of it showing up, physically, while we try to reach you emotionally.

B is INCORRECT
This may be a secondary issue but it is certainly not reserved for Asian American as a group. Most people feel a little shame at going to therapy because we are all taught that we need to handle ourselves. This is part of the American "Pull yourself up by your bootstraps" MYTH.

D is INCORRECT
For obvious reasons (smile)

Question 125   Section: CULTURAL

The correct answer is A
Amok – is a dissociative episode: period of brooding followed by an outburst of violent, aggressive or homicidal behavior directed at people and objects. Episode is precipitated by a perceived slight or insult. Episode is often accompanied by persecutory ideas, automatism, amnesia, exhaustion, and a return to premorbid state following the episode. Originally described in Malaysia. Similar episodes are found in Laos, Philippines, Polynesia, Papua New Guinea, Puerto Rico (mal de pelea), and among the Navajo (iich'aa)

If he was from West Africa or Haiti you would call this same behavior: boufée delirante - a cultural interaction from West Africa and Haiti. Sudden outburst of agitated and aggressive behavior, marked confusion, and psychomotor excitement. Sometimes accompanied by visual and auditory hallucinations or paranoid ideation. It may resemble a brief psychotic disorder.

B is INCORRECT

Because he is from New Guinea, it should be treated as a cultural syndrome and not as a psychotic disorder.

C is INCORRECT
dhat - folk diagnostic term used in India to refer to severe anxiety and hypochondriacal concerns associated with the discharge of semen, whitish discoloration of the urine, and feelings of weakness and exhaustion.

D is INCORRECT
Hwa-byung - Korean folk syndrome literally translated into English as "anger syndrome" and attributed to the suppression of anger. The symptoms include insomnia, fatigue, panic, fear of impending death, dysphoric affect, indigestion, anorexia, dyspnea, palpitations, generalized aches and pains.

CLINCIAL NOTE: You do not have to memorize all the different cultural syndromes. Just be aware when assessing a person from another culture or country that behavior we might consider to be problematic is culturally acceptable.

Question 126   Section: CLINICAL

The correct answer is C
Autistic fantasy occurs when a client copes with emotional conflict or internal/external stressors by excessively daydreaming, instead of seeking human relationships. Isolation is a more effective strategy for them than meeting and making new friends. When dealing with this kind of defense mechanism, probably your most effective strategy would be to give homework assignments that require the client to go into the community and do a specific task, which may involve other people. Also realize that part of the isolation may be due to poorly developed social skills and some

"Direct Interaction" training may be required as a way of teaching her how to interact with others

A is INCORRECT
Rationalization occurs when the client copes with emotional conflict or internal/external stressors by concealing the true motivations for his or her own thoughts, actions, or feelings through the elaboration of reassuring or self-serving but incorrect explanations.

B is INCORRECT
projection occurs when a client copes with emotional conflict or internal/external stressors by falsely attributing to another his or her own unacceptable feelings, impulses, or thoughts.

D is INCORRECT
devaluation occurs when a client copes with emotional conflict or internal/external stressors by attributing exaggerated negative qualities to self or others

Question 127   Section: CLINICAL

The correct answer is B
idealization is used when the client copes with emotional conflict either internal or external, and internal/external stressors by attributing exaggerated positive qualities to others. It is often easier to see the world as perfect rather than perceive it as it is. This may be caused by a projection Saheed is using on the world, or it may cover up feelings of insecurity or even fear. If you believe everyone is great, you don't have to worry about them trying to hurt you, because they wouldn't. This defense mechanism is probably covering up a great deal of hurt and disappointment, so, as a therapist, I would not want to take it away very quickly. I would want to

fully explore the entire underbelly of the issue before I worked with Saheed to surrender this set of protections.

A is INCORRECT
Intellectualization is used by a client to cope with emotional conflict or internal/external stressors by the excessive use of abstract thinking or the making of generalizations to control or minimize disturbing feelings. This is often a very difficult defense mechanism to overcome because the individual will have probably learned some basic logic skills and will fight to maintain this perception. This is a defense mechanism that allows the user to feel "in control" because of its power at evading issues using logic. This is a defense mechanism that could take many sessions to confront fully.

C is INCORRECT
Humor is used to avoid problems. The client will use this to cope with almost all situations. They tend to emphasize the amusing or ironic aspects of the conflict or stressors. This is also a difficult mechanism to overcome. It can be used in many different situations to repel unwanted contact and to control a situation. The entire cast of Seinfeld is a glowing (if not somewhat exaggerated) example of people who are seriously maladaptive and use humor to avoid coping with their problems.

D is INCORRECT
Isolation of affect is a mechanism that allows the client to cope with emotional conflict or internal/ external stressors by separating their ideas from the feelings associated with them. Social skills training and changing expectations are both ways to deal with this defense mechanism in therapy.

Question 128   Section: CLINICAL

The correct answer is B
affiliation occurs when the client copes with emotional conflict or internal/ or external stress by turning to others for help or support. They will often share their problems with others. They usually do not try to make someone else responsible for their problems. It is important to note that ego defense mechanisms are neutral, and the pathology lies in how they are used. In this situation, there is no clear indication that her use of this mechanisms interferes with her social, emotional, or occupational functioning. Therefore there is no identified problem. It is clear that her family does not understand or like her responses, and this may indicate the need to educate the mother and father about the mechanism.

A is INCORRECT
acting out occurs when the client copes with emotional conflict or internal/external stress by actions rather than reflections or feelings. This definition is broader than the original concept of the acting out of transference, feelings or wishes during psychotherapy. This is intended to include behavior arising both within the psychotherapeutic transference as well as outside the dynamic relationship. Sometimes acting out is "defensive". This should not be confused with "bad behavior". It is defensive acting out because there is evidence that the behavior is related to emotional conflicts.

C is INCORRECT
altruism occurs when the client copes with emotional conflict or internal/external stress by dedicating themselves to the needs of others and to meet the needs of others. Unlike the self-sacrifice sometimes characteristic of reaction formation, the individual receives gratification either vicariously or from the

response of others. This may be part of the underpinning of the Munchausen's' Syndrome by Proxy.

D is INCORRECT
anticipation occurs when the client cope with emotional conflict or internal/external stress by experiencing emotional reactions in advance of, or anticipating consequences of, possible future events and considering realistic, alternative responses or solutions.

Question 129   Section: CLINICAL

The correct answer is B
Projective identification is a form of projection in which the client copes with emotional conflict or internal/external stressors by falsely attributing his or her own unacceptable feelings, impulses, or thoughts to someone else Unlike simple projection, the client does not fully deny his projection and often remains aware of his or her own affects or impulses, however they often falsely attribute then as justifiable reactions to the other persons behavior. Often, the client will induce or create the impulse in others, for the very feelings they mistakenly believe exist, which causes further problems in deciding who did what to whom first.

A is INCORRECT
passive aggression occurs when the client copes with emotional conflict or internal/external stress by indirectly and unassertively expressing aggression toward others. Often they present with a façade of overt compliance which masks serious covert resistance, hostility and resentment. Passive aggression often exhibits itself in response to demands for independence, freedom of action and/or performance of non-dependent behavior. It is often seen in situations where a person in a

subordinate position has no other safe method of expressing their assertiveness more openly and independently.

C is INCORRECT
reaction formation occurs when the client copes with emotional conflict or internal/external stress by substituting behavior, thoughts, or feelings that are diametrically opposed to their own unacceptable feelings or thoughts. You will often see the client repress these unacceptable feelings as a method of achieving cognitive consonance.

D is INCORRECT
repression occurs when the client copes with emotional conflict or internal/ external stress by expelling or pushing disturbing wishes, thoughts, or experiences from their conscious awareness. Often the feelings associated with the disturbing wishes, etc, remain in the conscious realm of the client, therefore causing emotional problems, while the actual associated ideas are pushed out of the conscious "light".

Question 130   Section: CLINICAL

The correct answer is C
Sublimation occurs when the individual copes with emotional conflict or internal/external stress by channeling potentially maladaptive feelings and impulses into socially acceptable behavior. Instead of venting his anger towards his daughter he sublimates it into "spreading the word" of his views to different churches.

A is INCORRECT
self-assertion occurs when the client copes with emotional conflict or stress by expressing their feelings and thoughts directly, in a non- coercive or non-manipulative manner.

B is INCORRECT

self-observation occurs when the client copes with emotional conflict or stress by reflecting on their own thoughts, feelings, motivation, and behavior, and responding appropriately.

D is INCORRECT

Suppression occurs when a client copes with emotional conflict or internal/external stress by intentionally avoiding thinking about disturbing problems, wishes, feelings, or experiences.

Question 131   Section: CLINICAL

The correct answer is D

The "help-rejecting" client copes with emotional conflict or internal/external stressors by complaining or making repetitious requests for help that mask or disguise buried feelings of hostility or reproach toward others.   They then reject suggestions, advice and offers of help.   Their complaints can be physical in nature or psychological.   Their secondary payback appears to be a self-reinforcing loop of "I can't be helped and I can't change my environment, so I am justified in feeling anxious and pressured."

This particular ego-defense mechanism can be approached with basic reality therapy; "What do you want?"; "Are you getting what you want?"; "Is what you're getting making you happy?"

This approach transfers the onus of responsibility for the problems back on the client and renders the defense mechanism avoid. At this point they will either begin to change or will find a therapist who wants to play their "game.'

A is INCORRECT

Denial is used by the client to cope with emotional conflict or internal/external stress by refusing to acknowledge painful aspects of their external reality or of their subjective experience.   Usually this external reality of subjective experience is apparent to others.

B is INCORRECT
Displacement manifests itself when the client copes with emotional conflict or internal/external stress by transferring feelings about one object onto another object.   Usually the object the feelings are transferred to is less threatening or scary than the object avoided.
(It is safe to yell at your children and may be dangerous to yell at your boss, even though the boss is causing you stress.)

C is INCORRECT
Dissociation is seen when the client copes with emotional conflict or internal/external stress with a breakdown in their integration of the functions of consciousness, memory, perception of self,   the environment, and/or sensory-motor behavior.

Question 132   Section: CLINICAL

The correct answer is B
Emotional reasoning is a thinking error where you ASSUME that your negative feelings are TRUE, without any direct evidence to support them.   This thinking error has an "emotional payoff". The payoff comes in the form of you not having to review your feelings and compare them to the accurate facts. You get to maintain your belief system without putting any energy into change. You also are able to avoid any real criticism of your refusal to change.

A is INCORRECT

Entitlement is the thinking error where you BELIEVE you have suffered and that LIFE now OWES you. It allows you to cope with mistakes by believing that people should cut you some slack because you are a victim and they should understand that you only made the mistake BECAUSE you are A VICTIM. This thinking error allows you to relieve yourself of any responsibility or guilt for your actions.

C is INCORRECT
Fortune telling is the thinking error where you BELIEVE you possess the power to see the future and the future is BAD. Because it is always bad, there is no particular reason to change your behavior...because it will not matter. You feel anyone who is optimistic or has hope for the future is simply uninformed.

D is INCORRECT
Externalization is the thinking error that allows you to BELIEVE that all human suffering is caused by external events and the only way you can control your life is to control all events in your life. This thinking error allows you to claim yourself as a victim of circumstance and removes your need to change, because you are not in control anyway.

Question 133   Section: CLINICAL

The correct answer is C
Jumping to conclusions is a thinking error or pattern of erroneous thought which allows the adolescent to interpret a situation negatively, regardless of any external evidence to support their beliefs. This allows Tommy to always be right because he does not have to gather information or ask others for feedback.

A is INCORRECT

Image is a thinking error which occurs when the client is trying to copy other people because they do not feel they have a "true self." They do not know who they are and therefore will mimic other people. As a clinician you have to be careful about this error because it closely parallels the conflict in the Ericksonian Stage of Identity VS Role Confusion. Some copying behavior is to be expected in adolescents, however, when it becomes the primary mechanism, you will begin to see problems. If Tommy were using IMAGE he would be very involved in something and dressing or acting like that "something" all the time.

B is INCORRECT
When your client is catastrophizing, they only see the worst of everything. They will take any negative and stretch it to the farthest ends of perception. This thinking error allows the client to stop trying because they will never be successful. It allows them to cease trying. If Tommy were catastrophizing, he would talk about how bad it was going to each of the events he was invited to.

D is INCORRECT
The client who uses MIND READING actively believes they know what other people are thinking by their actions and what the other person thinks about them is bad. They do not bother to ask the person whose "mind" they are reading for clarification. This allows them to plead a lack of control in their lives and they should not be held responsible. If Tommy were MIND READING, he would be telling you "his parents hate him" or "he knows they are mad at him."

Question 134   Section: CLINICAL

The correct answer is B

Using the victim stance allows you to blame other people for what has happened to you. Your primary behavioral mechanism is to "point fingers at others" and "generate excuses" for your lack of success. The pay-off for this type of behavior is the ability to NOT ACCEPT responsibility for your life. There is no need to put in the hard work of actually determining why you are "where you are".

Other examples of statements that show this thinking error are:

1) The thief who says, "He (the victim) is the real criminal here. His watch only cost $75 and the court is making me pay restitution of $250.
2) I do what I do because my father was a drunk. If he had cared about me and stopped drinking, I would not be like I am.
3) My boss pays me minimum wage. I broke into his car because I needed some extra money. If people are going to pay such low wages, they got to expect I will have to steal to survive."

A is INCORRECT
The "Good person" stance is a thinking error that belongs to a class of BLACK and WHITE views of the world. You often see this type of behavior in people who have been diagnosed with a personality disorder.
You are the good guy, no matter what you do. You see all behavior in terms of you being in the "right" and other people being in the "wrong". There is no GREY in your universal view. You actively ignore anything which does not fit nicely into your world view.

C is INCORRECT
The "Lack-of-time" stance is a thinking error which focused only on the HERE and NOW. The person who used this stance will

refuse to look at the past and will not be willing to explain past behaviors. They only are interested in their current needs and wants. These people often expect to be a big success without any effort. Common statements you may hear during a session are "You only live once" and "if I don't get it now, I may never get it."

D is INCORRECT
This thinking error has a lot in common with the ego defense mechanism of ENTITLEMENT. You believe that there is no one in the world like you, or that your experiences are unique among people and therefore you have a right to do what you want because the rules don't apply to you. This also plays into the feelings of superiority of your feelings because "you believe you will never get caught."

Question 135   Section: CLINICAL

The correct answer is A
The fragmented personality thinking error is common in persons with antisocial features. It is a method where they can interpersonal conflict by separating themselves into two personality sets. They have a core belief that they are a good person and therefore could do no wrong. If they do something exploitive or hurtful they can justify it by making the logical leap: "If I am a good person and I hurt someone, they must have done something to deserve it, because I would not hurt them for no reason. They caused it. It has nothing to do with whether or not I am a good person." This thinking error allows them to refuse to look at the inconsistency between their beliefs and actions.

B IS INCORRECT

Justifying is also an externalizing thinking error. It allows the user to place all blame outside of them and therefore be able to avoid responsibility. Statements you may hear which could clue you in on this error would include: "He yelled at me so I had a right to hit him."; "She was mean to me so I broke her pottery."

C is INCORRECT
Fronting occurs when the client creates a persona which they use to try to convince you they are something or someone they are not. This error is similar to a conscious splitting where they can deny behaviors they have committed by refusing or denying they committed the behaviors. This error responds well to a simple statement that you know they are fronting and they should stop.

D IS INCORRECT
A person using the thinking error "Grandiosity" often has an exaggerated sense of self-importance or ability. They often feel they are the best or the best at doing something. They refuse to process any of their actions which could conflict with this thinking pattern. This client is minimizing or maximizing the significance of an issue, and it justifies not solving the problem.

Statements you may hear from a client involved in this thinking error may include:
> "I hate school; I could run the classroom better than that stupid teacher."

> "Coach is stupid; I am a better player than him. I should be playing Quarterback!"

Question 136   Section: ETHICAL

The correct answer is D

[111]

This is a very complex situation. The answer here is not so much an ethical consideration as it is a concern for you and your current licensure status. In the state of Florida, you are considered to be a licensed individual. However you are licensed as a Clinical Social Worker intern. In other states you would be licensed as a Master Social Worker. Both of these licensure designations are non-independent. Which means, in order for you to work, your license is tied to, and subordinate to, an Independent License, held by your Licensed Clinical Social Work Supervisor. Your license is not recognized as a license to practice independently. Assuming the information you have is correct, the ex-wife carries an independent license. The short answer here is that regardless of your expertise, regardless of your experience, and regardless of your competency, your license is not as powerful as the license of an independent clinical social worker. In any possible confrontation you will be seen as a subordinate, and as an intern. Numerous situations involving the custody arrangements of children become very contentious between all parties. There is a high probability that if you continue with this case you will be involved in some contentious situation with both parties. It would be very easy for the ex-wife to "pull rank on you" in a licensure sense. It would be quite possible for you to injure your career or possibly your chance at independent licensure status if you were to continue working with this case. The most appropriate thing to do would be to turn the case over to your agency and have them assign a licensed professional.

A is INCORRECT.
While there is no specific ethical violation for seeing this couple in therapy, there is nothing positive that can come out of it for you. All relationships, as they breakup, can become volatile. People become angry and are looking for resolution and retribution. Whether you like it or not, there is a form of bigotry among licensed professionals. Fully independent licenses are

more powerful than intern licenses. And if a confrontation were to occur you would be placing your subordinate license against an independent license. Chances are very good you would lose. Even if you did not lose, you could end up in the middle of an investigation that could take several months to sort out all the particulars. The best thing you can do is to refer this back to your agency and walk away.

B is INCORRECT
The largest problem you will have been the situation, if you want to continue to provide services, would be to place yourself in an adversarial position between this divorcing couple. This would allow you to be triangulated between the two parties. If you were to choose to provide services to the husband only and ask that the month the wife receive a separate therapist, you would only be exacerbated the triangulation. You would also allow the couple to continue their fight through two different proxies, yourself and the other therapist.

C is INCORRECT
Whether the ex-wife wants a licensed clinician because she feels they would be able to better handle the situation, or because they felt that they might have more control over the clinician, it is highly unlikely that the wife is going on accept you as a clinical peer. She will probably see you as inferior in training and skill. No good can come to you in providing services in the situation. Refer the case back to your agency and walk away.

Question 137   Section: ETHICAL

The correct answer is B
This is a very complex situation. Your primary ethical responsibility is to the client.   It is to ensure they receive the correct and appropriate information they require to make

appropriate decisions for their adult child. You need to supply her with the correct information as well as interfering with the other MSW providing her with incorrect information. Needless to say, this should be done with tact. Something like, "I am not sure that is correct. I have called ... And was given different information." As long as you can quote the source of your information, and the time frame in which your information was gathered, you should be alright. If you keep the exchange professional, and do not let your irritation takeover, the mother will figure out who has the most correct information.

A is INCORRECT
if you simply ignore the incorrect information being given by the other professional, to the mother, you run the risk of allowing mother to leave the meeting with incorrect information which may well cause problems for your client, the traumatic brain injury adult female. You have to accept responsibility for ensuring in that mother gets the correct information. As a social worker, there are many times when you will have to be confrontational. The trick is to be confrontational in a tactful manner, this is professional, and ensures that all parties grow and learn from the experience.

C is INCORRECT
While at first glance, this may seem like the best answer, it is not. This answer allows you to avoid a confrontation with the other professional. Many times in your work you will have to be confrontational. You are, after all, at your core, an advocate for your clients. The danger in answering this way is that you run the risk of allowing the mother to leave the conference with inaccurate information. And if the mother does not reschedule, or reschedules and does not show up she may well have left the conference with inaccurate information. Your job is to make sure that she has the accurate information she needs.

D is INCORRECT

In any exchange, as a social worker you must maintain a professional demeanor. During the conference with the mother, your personal feelings are irrelevant. You have a mandate, as a social worker, to provide the client was accurate and appropriate information. There is no room for personal feelings, at this point in time.

This is not to say that your feelings are unimportant. Or that you should not feel hurt, angry, slighted or anyone of a number of other feelings. It simply means that as a professional social worker you need to separate your personal feelings from your professional work. There will be plenty of time, at a later date, to deal with the situation and your feelings.

Question 138   Section: ETHICAL

The correct answer is C

The secretary of the agency, since they are the representative for the agency the client is currently involved with, should contact the caller and instruct her that all information requests need to be in writing. Also the release of all information needs to be done after an informed consent for release information is provided by the client. Regardless of the involvement of the Department of children and families with your client, your primary goal is to facilitate growth and protect their confidentiality. Also because you have no involvement with the child and you know the child is a safe location. There is no particular information you have to give to the Department of family services.

A is INCORRECT

whether or not Judy is from the Department of Children and Family services, without proper authorization she has no access to the information that you have gathered on your client. If indeed, there is a court hearing or court involvement on this client, or her child, the attorney for DCF will be able to submit to you a subpoena asking for information and requesting your presence at a deposition or a hearing. Remember that all people, regardless of their position or station, who wish to have access to information on your clients, must come through standard channels. Your client drives therapy; your client also drives control of information. Your client is the only person who can determine what information is released, unless there is a court order, or a subpoena.

B is INCORRECT
technically the client belongs to the agency, or the drop in center. And you are the therapist. This is not a private practice client. You have no responsibility to return the call to Judy and give her the information. This is a task the agency should do. The agency may not be used to dealing with the department children and family, they may not be used to dealing with any outside agency. The agency must however, have policies and procedures for the release of confidential information.

D is INCORRECT
This answer is not correct, because it can leave your client open to some problems. If your client is indeed involved with the court systems, at some point in time you will probably have to interface with them. There is no benefit to your client for angering or frustrating the court system. However, you need to keep in mind that all information can only be released to specific channels, with specific agreements and paperwork. While no one could probably fault to you, for throwing away the number and not returning the call, you could end up causing your client grief and undermining your client's position on an issue that is very important to your client.

Question 139   Section: ETHICAL

The correct answer is A

Ethics are messy and they often seem like little things that will have no great consequence. However, they shape who we are. The data gathered indicates a diagnosis of Adjustment Disorder. It could, with exaggeration and a blind eye be morphed into PTSD, but at what cost to the client. An adjustment disorder is considered to be short-term, PTSD is often considered chronic. If you frame the problem as an adjustment disorder the client learns that when things happen to them they may have a reaction, but the situation is able to be overcome. They are likely to adopt that attitude. If you frame it as PTSD, they may frame it as chronic and invasive and accept it as a permanent part of themselves. They may come to identify with it and it may damage "who they are." These are not trivial things we deal with each day. Your need to get paid can never overshadow your client's long-term health. If the parents really want the girl to see you, they may be able to make arrangements. Remember, you are a therapist and clinician, not a savior.

B is INCORRECT

The moment you decide to give a diagnosis that is acceptable to an insurance company, rather than to the "truth" of the situation, you have bastardized yourself and your profession. We all work alone. No-one really knows what goes on in our offices or our heads. It is human nature (and very easy) to justify situations which we would not originally agree to do. As a rule of thumb, before you do something like this, ask yourself if you would be comfortable standing in a group of your peers and telling them you did this.

C is INCORRECT

The only thing more compromising than deciding to give a false or unsubstantiated diagnosis is to bring others into the situation and collaborate. You are not only willing to ignore your ethics but are also willing to talk other people into thing which are inappropriate. Realize, that while proving it may be very difficult and the possibility of being caught is remote, your behavior could be construed as insurance fraud.

D) You have already decided you cannot take on any more pro bono clients. You should have made this decision as a matter of workload versus money. If you do decide to change the decision and take on the client, be sure you are doing it for appropriate reasons and not to fulfill a need in yourself to be a savior or to try to "rescue" someone. This is the fast track to burnout.

Question 140   Section: ETHICAL

The correct answer is B
you must always remember that you are driven by the needs, and the wants of the client. The client is allowed to determine their status, their intervention, and every other aspect of treatment. You cannot force a client to do anything, except under very specialized circumstances. You are under no obligation to get the client to sign any financial paperwork. If the client refused to sign and your agency decides to terminate services, that situation is beyond your control. By the way, writing refused across the signature line indicates very clearly that you gave the client the option and the client chose to decline. It also proves you presented the paperwork to the client.

A is INCORRECT
demanding the client to sign anything could be seen as coercive. It could be declared unethical by your license board,

and certainly not in the best interest of the client. Your client has the right to determine the future. They have the right to make their financial decisions. It should also be noted that failure on the part of your agency to ensure that the financial paperwork was completed properly before seeing the client is not your mess to clean up.

C is INCORRECT
this would most certainly be seen as coercive. It also robs the client of their right to make a decision. While you probably cannot refuse to bring the paperwork to the client, without the risk of getting reprimanded or fired by the agency, the fact that you're asked to do something that should be done by administration, should make you think deeply. Why is your agency putting you in this position.

D is INCORRECT
while this certainly could be viewed as an ethical move on your part, it may cause problems with your employment with the agency down the road. Like most situations in life this situation has a formal and informal aspect. The informal aspect is to get paid. The formal aspect is to use your relationship with the client as a method of ensuring payment. If you refuse to do this, the company will probably fall back upon the belief that you were "simply asked to do a simple job" and that the company was not trying to take advantage of anybody. They would've been probably begun to question your loyalty to the company and may even ask you why you thought the company was trying to take advantage of anybody. It is a no-win situation for you. The best response is to present the paperwork to the client and if they refuse to sign it, explain to them how to do so appropriately.

Question 141   Section: CLINICAL

The correct answer is C
The DSM-IV classifies four distinct levels of mental retardation. These are (from most debilitating to least) Profound, Severe, Moderate, Mild.   Individuals with an IQ range of 35-55 are classified as having MODERATE Mental Retardation. They are generally able to learn communication skills during childhood. They can learn to carry out self-care and work tasks with moderate supervision and can often live a rather independent life in a supervised environment like a group home. Of the entire population of individuals with mental retardation, about 10% are classified as in this range.

A is INCORRECT
An IQ score between 20-40 generally indicate severe mental retardation.   This group of individuals make up about 3-4% of the population of individuals who suffer from Mental Retardation. They may learn to master basic self-care skills and very basic communication skills; however they will never achieve self-sufficiency.   These individuals may be able to live in a group home with constant supervision.

B is INCORRECT
Approximately 85% of the mentally retarded population is in the mildly retarded category. Their IQ score ranges from 50-75, and they can often acquire academic skills up to the 6th grade level. They can become fairly self-sufficient and in some cases live independently, with community and social support.

D is INCORRECT
Only 1-2% of the mentally retarded population is classified as profoundly retarded. Profoundly retarded individuals have IQ scores under 20-25. They may be able to develop basic self-care and communication skills with appropriate support and

training. Their retardation is often caused by an accompanying neurological disorder. The profoundly retarded need a high level of structure and supervision.

The American Association on Mental Retardation (AAMR) has developed another widely accepted diagnostic classification system for mental retardation. The AAMR classification system focuses on the capabilities of the retarded individual rather than on the limitations. The categories describe the level of support required. They are: intermittent support, limited support, extensive support, and pervasive support. To some extent, the AAMR classification mirrors the DSM-IV classification. Intermittent support, for example, is support needed only occasionally, perhaps during times of stress or crisis. It is the type of support typically required for most mildly retarded individuals. At the other end of the spectrum, pervasive support, or life-long, daily support for most adaptive areas, would be required for profoundly retarded individuals.

Ref:http://medical-dictionary.thefreedictionary.com/
Moderate+mental+retardation

Question 142   Section: CLINICAL

The correct answer is B
Brain Lateralization Theory is the idea that the two halves of the brain's cerebral cortex -- left and right -- execute different functions. The lateralization theory -- developed by Nobel-prize-winners Roger Sperry and Robert Ornstein -- helps us to understand our behavior, our personality, our creativity, and our ability to use the proper mode of thinking when performing particular tasks. (The cerebral cortex is a part of the brain that exists only in humans and higher mammals, to manage our sophisticated intellect.)

The two halves ("hemispheres") are joined by the Corpus Collosum. This is a bundle of more than 200 million nerve fibers which transmit data from one hemisphere to the other so that the two halves can communicate. Although this nerve connection would seem to be vital, it is severed in a surgical procedure for some people who have epilepsy. The corpus collosum is up to 40 percent larger in women than it is in men.

We can specify the functions of the two hemispheres. (The following descriptions apply to right-handed people; for left-handed people, this information is reversed; for example, it is the right hemisphere which processes analytical thought.)

The left hemisphere specializes in analytical thought. The left hemisphere deals with hard facts: abstractions, structure, discipline and rules, time sequences, mathematics, categorizing, logic and rationality and deductive reasoning, knowledge, details, definitions, planning and goals, words (written and spoken and heard), productivity and efficiency, science and technology, stability, extraversion, physical activity, and the right side of the body. The left hemisphere is emphasized in our educational system and in our society in general, for better or for worse; as Marshall McLuhan speculated, "The day when bureaucracy becomes right hemisphere will be utopia."

The right hemisphere specializes in the "softer" aspects of life. This includes intuition, feelings and sensitivity, emotions, daydreaming and visualizing, creativity (including art and music), color, spatial awareness, first impressions, rhythm, spontaneity and impulsiveness, the physical senses, risk-taking, flexibility and variety, learning by experience, relationships, mysticism, play and sports, introversion, humor, motor skills, the left side of the body, and a holistic way of perception that recognizes patterns and similarities and then synthesizes those elements into new forms.

Ref::http://www.theorderoftime.com/politics/cemetery/
stout/h/brain-la.htm

A is INCORRECT
This is a "made up" phrase

C is INCORRECT
This is a "made up" phrase

D is INCORRECT
This is a "made up" phrase

Question 143   Section: CLINICAL

The Correct Answer is A
An EEG is an ElectroEncephaloGraph, and is used to measure alpha waves activity in the brain. These waves occur when we are both alert and relaxed. These waves decrease with concentrated or busy activity. They have been studied in depression and relaxation.

B is INCORRECT
I don't know what this one is but if you ever find something that does this, please forward it to me. It could provide information for many dissertations.

C is INCORRECT
The concept of Mental Retardation caused by an extra chromosome is known as Trisomy 21. It goes by the common name of Down's Syndrome.

D is INCORRECT
Not directly! We definitely could benefit from knowing more about the physiology of our bodies, but that research is probably 20 years off.

Question 144   Section: CLINICAL

The Correct Answer is A

Smoking is linked to lower birth weights and premature birth rates. Children born to women who smoke are at risk for the following other possibilities as well: 1) "According to Marjorie Greenfield, M.D. at DrSpock.com, an overabundance of red blood cells in the fetus can cause a thickening of the blood, thus blocking blood flow. The carbon monoxide that is created when tobacco smoke is consumed displaces oxygen in the blood. This displacement can cause the fetus to produce more red blood cells to compensate for the lack of sufficient oxygen."

2) Nicotine is believed to contribute to behavioral and nervous disorders in newborn babies. This comes from the hypothesis that nicotine affects the production of neurotransmitters in the brain. Serotonin and dopamine are replaced by nicotine which causes withdraw symptoms after the baby is born.

3) Fetal Thyroid Damage - The thyroid gland, which begins to develop by the 12th week of gestation, is responsible for metabolism and growth rates. Smoking affects thyroid development in fetuses, which seems to cause neuron damage. This damage was seen as contributing to the potential for debilitating mental conditions such as retardation. This effect is caused by both first-hand and second-hand smoke.

Reference: http://www.ehow.com/about_5292686_effects-smoking-fetus.html

B is INCORRECT

There are many causes of mental retardation, including Trisomy 21, Anoxia, Alcohol Abuse and a variety of abused substances. Given our current store of knowledge, smoking is not a primary cause of mental retardation.

C is INCORRECT

There is no direct correlation in the research showing a link between muscle tone at birth and smoking.

D is INCORRECT

Tay Sachs is a genetic disorder which tends to show itself in Eastern European populations and their descendants, especially Ashkenazic Jews. It is initially debilitating and finally fatal in all cases by age 6-7. The only "cure" is the testing of the parents for the recessive trait and genetic counseling regarding transmission of the double recessive gene during conception.

Question 145   Section: CLINICAL

The Correct Answer is D

These parents show a permissive style of parenting. Permissive parents, sometimes referred to as indulgent parents, have very few demands to make of their children. These parents rarely discipline their children because they have relatively low expectations of maturity and self-control. According to Baumrind, permissive parents "are more responsive than they are demanding. They are nontraditional and lenient, do not require mature behavior, allow considerable self-regulation, and avoid confrontation" (1991). Permissive parents are generally nurturing and communicative with their children, often taking on the status of a friend more than that of a parent.

Baumrind found the impact of permissive parenting often results in children who rank low in happiness and self-regulation. These children are more likely to experience problems with authority and tend to perform poorly in school.

A is INCORRECT

In this style of parenting, children are expected to follow the strict rules established by the parents. Failure to follow such rules usually results in punishment. Authoritarian parents fail to explain the reasoning behind these rules. If asked to explain, the parent might simply reply, "Because I said so." These parents have high demands, but are not responsive to their children. According to Baumrind, these parents "are obedience- and status-oriented, and expect their orders to be obeyed without explanation" (1991).

B is INCORRECT
Like authoritarian parents, those with an authoritative parenting style establish rules and guidelines that their children are expected to follow. However, this parenting style is much more democratic. Authoritative parents are responsive to their children and willing to listen to questions. When children fail to meet the expectations, these parents are more nurturing and forgiving rather than punishing. Baumrind suggests that these parents "monitor and impart clear standards for their children's conduct. They are assertive, but not intrusive and restrictive. Their disciplinary methods are supportive, rather than punitive. They want their children to be assertive, as well as socially responsible, and self-regulated as well as cooperative" (1991). Baumrind found the impact of authoritive parenting styles tend to result in children who are happy, capable and successful (Maccoby, 1992).

C is INCORRECT
An uninvolved parenting style is characterized by few demands, low responsiveness and little communication. While these parents fulfill the child's basic needs, they are generally detached from their child's life. In extreme cases, these parents may even reject or neglect the needs of their children. Baumrind found the impact of uninvolved parenting styles rank lowest across all life domains. These children tend to lack self-control, have low self-esteem and are less competent than their peers.
http://psychology.about.com/od/developmentalpsychology/a/pa renting-style.htm

Question 146   Section: HUMAN DIVERSITY

The Correct Answer is A
The primary tenet of Social Work is the right of client self-determination. Even if the client does not agree with you, or chooses to live in a manner which you consider to be inappropriate or degrading. As long as they are not a danger to themselves or others, they are free to make their own decisions.

B is INCORRECT
If she asked you to do this, you should comply. She would be directing her behavior, however, this is not a part of the question and cannot be assumed.

C is INCORRECT
There is nothing in the scenario that tells you about her family.

D is INCORRECT
You should do this with her or after she leaves, and be ready to suggest alternatives when she comes by again. Except in very extreme circumstances, you are required to allow the client the right of self-control and choice.

Question 147   Section: CLINICAL

The correct answer is A
-- School Age: 6 to 12 Years
-- Ego Development Outcome: Industry vs. Inferiority
-- Basic Strengths: Method and Competence
During this stage, often called the Latency, we are capable of learning, creating and accomplishing numerous new skills and knowledge, thus developing a sense of industry. This is also a very social stage of development and if we experience unresolved feelings of inadequacy and inferiority among our

peers, we can have serious problems in terms of competence and self-esteem.

As the world expands a bit, our most significant relationship is with the school and neighborhood. Parents are no longer the complete authorities they once were, although they are still important.

http://www.learningplaceonline.com/stages/organize/Erikson.htm

B is INCORRECT
-- Young adulthood: 18 to 35
-- Ego Development Outcome: Intimacy and Solidarity vs Isolation
-- Basic Strengths: Affiliation and Love

In the initial stage of being an adult we seek one or more companions and love. As we try to find mutually satisfying relationships, primarily through marriage and friends, we generally also begin to start a family, though this age has been pushed back for many couples who today don't start their families until their late thirties. If negotiating this stage is successful, we can experience intimacy on a deep level. If we're not successful, isolation and distance from others may occur. And when we don't find it easy to create satisfying relationships, our world can begin to shrink as, in defense, we can feel superior to others.

Our significant relationships are with marital partners and friends.

http://www.webster.edu/~woolflm/lrerikson.html

C is INCORRECT
The final stage of Erikson's (1982) theory is later adulthood (age 60 years and older). The crisis represented by this last life stage is integrity versus despair. Erikson (1982) proposes that this stage begins when the individual experiences a sense of

mortality. This may be in response to retirement, the death of a spouse or close friends, or may simply result from changing social roles. No matter what the cause, this sense of mortality precipitates the final life crisis. The final life crisis manifests itself as a review of the individual1s life-career. Similar to Butler's (1963) life review, individuals review their life-career to determine if it was a success or failure. According to Erikson (1982), this reminiscence or introspection is most productive when experienced with significant others. The outcome of this life-career reminiscence can be either positive or negative. Ego integrity is the result of the positive resolution of the final life crisis. Ego integrity is viewed as the key to harmonious personality development; the individual views their whole of life with satisfaction and contentment. The ego quality that emerges from a positive resolution is wisdom. Erikson (1982) defines wisdom as a kind of "informed and detached concern with life itself in the face of death itself" (p. 61). Conversely, despair is the result of the negative resolution or lack of resolution of the final life crisis. This negative resolution manifests itself as a fear of death, a sense that life is too short, and depression. Despair is the last dystonic element in Erikson's (1959, 1982) theory.
Reference: http://www.webster.edu/~woolflm/lrerikson.html

D is INCORRECT
-- Adolescence: 12 to 18 Years
-- Ego Development Outcome: Identity vs. Role Confusion
-- Basic Strengths: Devotion and Fidelity

Up to this stage, according to Erikson, development mostly depends upon what is done to us. From here on out, development depends primarily upon what we do. And while adolescence is a stage at which we are neither a child nor an adult, life is definitely getting more complex as we attempt to find our own identity, struggle with social interactions, and grapple with moral issues.

Our task is to discover who we are as individuals separate from our family of origin and as members of a wider society. Unfortunately, for those around us, in this process many of us go into a period of withdrawing from responsibilities, which Erikson called a "moratorium." And if we are unsuccessful in navigating this stage, we will experience role confusion and upheaval.

A significant task for us is to establish a philosophy of life and in this process we tend to think in terms of ideals, which are conflict free, rather than reality, which is not. The problem is that we don't have much experience and find it easy to substitute ideals for experience. However, we can also develop strong devotion to friends and causes. It is no surprise, that our most significant relationships are with peer groups.

Reference: http://www.learningplaceonline.com/stages/organiz e/Erikson.htm

Question 148   Section: CLINICAL

The correct answer is B
Boundaries lead to differentiation of roles and tasks in a community setting. In general, boundaries are a very good thing to help individuals to structure their relationships. Some level of boundaries are essential to proper development. Enmeshment is a lack of boundaries and an intermingling of roles and responsibilities. This often leads to confusion and conflict.

A is INCORRECT
Lack of boundaries would create more enmeshment

C is INCORRECT
Boundaries should always change a level of enmeshment

D is INCORRECT
Differentiation is a the opposite side of the enmeshment coin

Question 149   Section: CLINICAL

The correct answer is C
Cognitive dissonance is an uncomfortable feeling caused by holding conflicting ideas simultaneously. The theory of cognitive dissonance proposes that people have a motivational drive to reduce dissonance. They do this by changing their attitudes, beliefs, and actions. Dissonance is reduced by justifying, blaming, and denying. It is one of the most influential and extensively studied theories in social psychology. A closely related term, cognitive disequilibrium, was coined, by Jean Piaget to refer to the experience of a discrepancy between something new and something already known or believed.
Reference: http://en.wikipedia.org/wiki/Cognitive_dissonance

A is INCORRECT
Dissociation is a partial or complete disruption of the normal integration of a person's conscious or psychological functioning. Dissociation can be a response to trauma or drugs and perhaps allows the mind to distance itself from experiences that are too much for the psyche to process at that time. Dissociative disruptions can affect any aspect of a person's functioning. Although some dissociative disruptions involve amnesia, the vast majority of dissociative events do not. Since dissociations are normally unanticipated, they are typically experienced as startling, autonomous intrusions into the person's usual ways of responding or functioning. Due to their unexpected and largely inexplicable nature, they tend to be quite unsettling.
Reference: http://en.wikipedia.org/wiki/Dissociation

B is INCORRECT

Acculturation is the exchange of cultural features that results when groups of individuals having different cultures come into continuous first hand contact. The original cultural patterns of either or both groups may be altered, but the groups remain.
Reference: http://en.wikipedia.org/wiki/Acculturation

D is INCORRECT

In developmental psychology - particularly analytical psychology - individuation is the process through which a person becomes his/her 'true self'. Hence it is the process whereby the innate elements of personality; the different experiences of a person's life and the different aspects and components of the immature psyche become integrated over time into a well-functioning whole. Individuation might thus be summarized as the stabilizing of the personality.
Reference: http://en.wikipedia.org/wiki/Individuation

Question 150   Section: ETHICS

The correct answer is C
There is no indication that the professionals involved made any mistakes in their assessment of the mental state of Poddar or in understanding what he was capable of doing.

A brief description of the case follows:
On October 27, 1969, Prosenjit Poddar killed Tatiana Tarasoff. Tatiana's parents alleged that two months earlier Poddar confided his intention to kill Tatiana to Dr. Lawrence Moore, a psychologist employed by the Cowell Memorial Hospital at the University of California at Berkeley. Dr. Moore requested the campus police detain Poddar, and after a brief detention, they released him when they decided he appeared rational. Tatiana's parents have further stated that Dr. Harvey

Powelson, Moore's superior, then directed that no further action be taken to detain Poddar. No one warned Tatiana of Poddar's threats.

A is INCORRECT
Malpractice liability is directly affected by the Tarasoff case. You, as a mental health professional, have a DUTY to warn someone of a threat against their person or safety; thus allowing them to determine the credibility of the threat.

B is INCORRECT
Tarasoff directly defines the limits of Privileged communication. If your client threatens someone you can identify and you feel the threat is credible, then that part of the conversation with your client is no longer privileged and you have a duty to warn the person threatened.

D is INCORRECT
Tarasoff directly impacts what information can and cannot remain protected and confidential.

Question 151   Section: CLINICAL

The Correct answer is B
Diagnostic criteria for 301.83 Borderline Personality Disorder :
A pervasive pattern of instability of interpersonal relationships, self-image, and affects, and marked impulsivity beginning by early adulthood and present in a variety of contexts, as indicated by five (or more) of the following:
(1) frantic efforts to avoid real or imagined abandonment.
 Note: Do not include suicidal or self-mutilating behavior covered in Criterion 5.
(2) a pattern of unstable and intense interpersonal relationships characterized by alternating between extremes of idealization and devaluation

(3) identity disturbance: markedly and persistently unstable self-   image or sense of self
(4) impulsivity in at least two areas that are potentially self-damaging (e.g., spending, sex, Substance Abuse, reckless driving, binge eating).
Note: Do not include suicidal or self-mutilating behavior covered in Criterion 5.
(5) recurrent suicidal behavior, gestures, or threats, or self-mutilating behavior
(6) affective instability due to a marked reactivity of mood (e.g., intense episodic dysphoria, irritability, or anxiety usually lasting a few hours and only rarely more than a few days)
(7) chronic feelings of emptiness
(8) inappropriate, intense anger or difficulty controlling anger (e.g., frequent displays of   temper, constant anger, recurrent physical fights)
(9) transient, stress-related paranoid ideation or severe dissociative symptoms

A is INCORRECT
This behavioral set corresponds to the diagnostic criteria for 301.50 Histrionic Personality Disorder. A pervasive pattern of excessive emotionality and attention seeking, beginning by early adulthood and present in a variety of contexts,

C is INCORRECT

This behavioral set corresponds to the diagnostic criteria for 301.81 Narcissistic Personality Disorder. A pervasive pattern of grandiosity (in fantasy or behavior), need for admiration, and lack of empathy, beginning by early adulthood and present in a variety of contexts. Grandiosity is defined as inflated self-esteem or self-worth, usually manifested as content of thinking or talk with themes reflecting the patient's belief that he or she is the greatest or has special attributes or abilities.

D is INCORRECT
This behavioral set corresponds to the diagnostic criteria for 301.6 Dependent Personality Disorder. A pervasive and excessive need to be taken care of that leads to submissive and clinging behavior and fears of separation, beginning by early adulthood and present in a variety of contexts.

Question 152   Section: CLINICAL

The correct answer is B
Ontogenesis is defined as the process of an individual organism growing organically; a purely biological unfolding of events involved in an organism changing gradually from a simple to a more complex level. In psychoanalysis it is the process during which personality and sexual behavior mature through a series of stages: first oral stage and then anal stage and then phallic stage and then latency stage and finally genital stage.
Ref: http://www.thefreedictionary.com/ontogenesis

A is INCORRECT
Any word ending in -GENESIS described a process of creation or growth throughout a set period of time. Stimulation of an emotional state or arousal occurs from environmental and internal cues and is regarded as a response mechanism.

C is INCORRECT
It defines a symptom.

D is INCORRECT
Understanding the perceptions of your client and their interactions with their family are both extremely important to counseling. However, this answer deals with the "present" and ONTOGENESIS deals with the complete spectrum.

Question 153   Section: CLINICAL

The correct answer is B
Schizophreniform disorder replicates the Schizophrenia criteria but the duration symptoms exist are present between one and six months. Because you have no prior history of any symptoms, you cannot diagnose schizophrenia.

A is INCORRECT
The schizoid personality disorder is not related schizophrenia, even though it uses the same root word. Schizoid Personality Disorder is characterized by a long-standing pattern of detachment from social relationships. A person with schizoid personality disorder often has difficulty expression emotions and does so typically in very restricted range, especially when communicating with others

C is INCORRECT
A diagnosis of schizophrenia requires at least 2 of the following symptoms:, which must be present for a period of time of more than 6 months.

-Delusions
-Hallucinations
-Disorganized   speech   (e.g.,   frequent   derailment   or incoherence)

-Grossly disorganized or catatonic behavior
-Negative symptoms (e.g., a "flattening" of one's emotions, alogia, avolition)
(Only one symptom is required if delusions are bizarre or hallucinations consist of a voice keeping up a running commentary on the person's behavior or thoughts, or two or more voices conversing with each other.)

D is INCORRECT
Schizophrenia, undifferentiated Type is a category of schizophrenia in which we place individuals with symptoms that are not compatible with the other categories of schizophrenia. (I have always thought this diagnosis should be called Schizophrenia NOS)

Question 154   Section: ETHICS

The correct answer is D
Once you begin an intake you have an ethical obligation to assist the client. This obligation can be fulfilled by seeing the client for free (pro bono) or by reducing your fees (sliding scale) or by assuring a referral and a linkage (making sure the referral agency is contacted). The one thing you cannot do is to leave them stranded.

A is INCORRECT
This would be the same as throwing them out of your office. It could also be construed as client abandonment. Failure to pay does not give you the right to terminate services without an appropriate referral.

B is INCORRECT
This answer smacks of coercion and manipulation. You need to respect what the client brings to the table. They may not be good money managers, but helping them figure out how to

borrow money to see you would probably put you on the wrong side of an ethical complaint.

C is INCORRECT
This answer is analogous to C

Question 155   Section: CLINICAL

The Correct answer is C
The cognitive damage that is done by sexual abuse often leads to inappropriate and unstable relations. This may be due to the damage to normal societal boundaries. It may also be due to the feeling of being unprotected, and "out-of-control" which are part of the pattern of sexual abuse. Without healthy boundaries and healthy interactions with adults during the formative years, children are doomed to a life of discontent and disaster in their primary relationships.

A is INCORRECT.
While sexual dysfunction may occur as an adjunct to their abuse, it is not as highly correlated with sexual abuse as answer c. There are many causes of sexual dysfunction, and in reality, the term sexual dysfunction is too broad to be useful in this context.

B is INCORRECT
There is no direct correlation with alcohol abuse, alcoholism and sexual abuse survivors. While, it is possible that, alcohol may be used to cope with the stress and intrusive thoughts surrounding sexual trauma, it would most likely only become a problem if it were the primary escape mechanism used by the individual.

D is INCORRECT

While this is a possible outcome, there is not a high degree of correlation between this response and sexual abuse. That is to say; not everyone who is abused replicates the pattern.

Question 156   Section: CLINICAL

The correct answer is B
Dysthymia is a subcategory of depression. It is usually long-term, low level (not completely debilitating) and is experiences for years.

Clients with dysthymia will often display a low, dark, or sad mood on most days for at least 2 years. When dysthymia is diagnosed in children, it is possible the depression will present as irritability. You will almost always see two or more of the following symptoms present during the duration of the dysthymic state. These include 1) Feelings of hopelessness 2) Too little or too much sleep 3) Low energy or fatigue 4) Low self-esteem 5)   Poor appetite or overeating and 6) Poor concentration.   Also your client with dysthymia will have a negative self-view and will perceive their future as discouraging, as well as taking a dim view of other peoples life and life events.

A is INCORRECT
Hallucinations are more closely associated with psychotic disorders. A note of concern when dealing with olfactory hallucinations; olfactory means "sense of smell" and these types of hallucinations tend to be rare. They also have a tentative relationship with certain types of brain tumors. If you have a client complaining of olfactory hallucinations, it would be good practice to refer them for a diagnostic evaluation by a neurologist.

C is INCORRECT

These symptoms represent drug dependency or drug abuse. Most substance abusers who deal with stimulants will not present with a pattern of dysthymia.

D) is INCORRECT
These symptoms more closely resemble Post Traumatic Stress Disorder and are not specifically tied to Dysthymia.

Question 157   Section: CLINICAL

The correct answer is A
The primary diagnostic issues with PTSD are the identification of the trauma incident, the presence of intrusive thoughts and flashbacks, and the time-frame of greater than 1 month of symptoms.

B is INCORRECT
There is no real value, from a clinical perspective, of knowing the length of time between the trauma and the onset of symptoms. Many of our ego defense mechanisms allow or create the suppression, denial or refusal of accepting what has occurred to us. These processes can skew the length of time between event and response.

C is INCORRECT
Somatization, the occurrence of tactile or physical symptoms, does not play a role in the diagnosis of PTSD or Acute Stress Disorder.

D is INCORRECT
The degree of trauma is individualized to each person. Some situations, which may cause you great trauma, may hardly impact someone else.

Question 158   Section: CLINICAL

The correct answer is D
While SSRI's tend to be excellent medications with less side effects than their predecessor, Tricyclics and MAOI's, they are NOT side-effect free. One of the most disturbing side-effects to some men is the sexual dysfunction which can express itself in a range from mild impairment to complete impairment. Males, age 18 to 45, on average, do not respond well to problems involving sexual dysfunction.

A is INCORRECT
NMS is a life- threatening neurological disorder most often caused by an adverse reaction to neuroleptic or antipsychotic drugs. It generally presents with muscle rigidity, fever, autonomic instability and cognitive changes such as delirium, and is associated with elevated creatine phosphokinase. (Thus, blood tests will show if it is present)

B is INCORRECT
All SSRI's are covered by all major insurance plans. They have been around long enough that almost all of them are available in a 'generic' formulation

C is INCORRECT
Some people experience a mild "compression of affect", where they describe feeling 'non-depressed but also not happy". This side effect will often go away over time.

Question 159   Section: Ethical

The correct answer is D
You bear responsibility because you are the supervisor. The intake worker bears responsibility because they are the direct service person and they failed to report back after making a

clinically incorrect decision. The agency employs you both and therefore shares liability.

A is INCORRECT
While you bear responsibility because you failed to follow-up, you may well have born responsibility even if you followed up and did not correct the problem.

B is INCORRECT
The intake worker failed to follow your directive, made a bad decision on their own, then failed to report their decision to you. They bear responsibility, however they are not the only one.

C is INCORRECT
The agency bears responsibility because it is the focal point of the issue and provides the service. They however share responsibility with multiple other people. This situation represents a complete breakdown of emergency protocol and a young girl died for it.

Question 160   Section: Ethical

The correct answer is A
Your primary obligation is to your client. We are a client centered professional. If your obligation to your client is in opposition to your agency, you need to bite the bullet and take the disapproval of your agency.

B is INCORRECT
Social advocacy is secondary to your client concerns

C is INCORRECT
Client centered only, first and foremost

D is INCORRECT

Social advocacy is always secondary to the needs of your client. You never sacrifice your client on the altar of societal need.

Question 161   Section: Clinical

The correct answer is C
Patients with depression have a greater probability of suicidal behavior than patients without depression, generally speaking, however, there is no clear indication of suicidal thoughts or ideations, but there has been no concrete indications they are not present and just not being brought up by the client. Without further data from the patient and therapy, there should be no change in your level of concern about suicidal potential.

A is INCORRECT
There is no indication of any increase in risk factors or issues. In fact, the information given would lead you to believe suicide has not been a central topic in therapy. There is no information presented that would allow you to assess, let alone alter, your assessment of suicidal potential.

B is INCORRECT
There is no indication of a decrease in any factors, risk or otherwise.

D is INCORRECT
While SSRI's tend to be appropriate medications for depression, there is the possibility of increased suicidal potential on SSRI's. Whether a client is on SSRI's or not, should not cause you to alter your suicidal assessment. Only data and facts should allow you to alter your suicidal assessment.

Question 162   Section: Clinical

The correct answer is D
One of the myths of suicide is the belief that talking about it will plant the idea. This is a MYTH. People who are contemplating suicide are in need of immediate intervention. By discussing the situation openly you are removing the societal TABOO that "we don't talk about that." The "trick" is not to be judgmental. It is much easier for a therapist to have a dialogue with a client if they have had the dialogue with themselves.

Personal Hint: My belief is that almost everyone has thought about suicide at some point. Making peace with this fact makes being non-judgmental, all the more, simple. Taboos need to be confronted directly. In my experience, when a person is contemplating suicide, they have run out of internal options. They have become "tunnel-visioned" and are unable to see opportunities. It has always been helpful to me to try to walk them through options, even if they have already dismissed them, because a new insight might occur.

A is INCORRECT
It is always a good idea to gather as much information as you can, and the genogram and eco-map will gather a lot if information, you must first confront he suicidal possibilities directly. This is a question that requires an "order of precedent"

B is INCORRECT
Once again, not a bad idea, but not the first thing you need to attend to.

C is INCORRECT
This is ABSOLUTELY WRONG in all circumstances. Never avoid talking to someone about suicide. Often people who contemplate suicide will feel their thoughts and ideas are too

strange to talk about. Remember, suicide is a process that continues when there is isolation, failure of coping mechanisms, and a very negative internal dialogue. If your client believes you will not want to talk about suicide, they will not talk openly. Discussing suicide normalizes their thought processes and allows them to talk about their feelings. People do not follow through with suicidal plans because they talk about suicide, they follow through because they feel alone and abandoned.

Final Thought: Most people think of suicide as passive and harming the individual only. In my experience suicide can be a very aggressive act. When someone is thinking, "They will miss me when I am gone!" or "This will show them!", these are aggressive thoughts. They are an attack on those that survive. Learn everything you can about suicide and challenge all your prejudices.

Question 163   Section: Clinical-Diagnostic

The correct answer is A
Korsakoff's syndrome goes by many names (Korsakoff's dementia, Korsakov's syndrome, Korsakoff's psychosis, or amnesic-confabulatory syndrome). It is a neurological disorder caused by the lack of thiamine (vitamin B1) in the brain. Its onset is linked to chronic alcohol abuse and/or severe malnutrition. (Alcohol has a lot of calories and chronic alcoholics can often get there calorie needs met by drinking, however, there are no vitamins and nutrients in alcohol, so eventually the person will suffer from severe nutrition.) The syndrome gets its name from the neuropsychiatrist who popularized the theory, Sergei Korsakoff.

The six major symptoms of Korsakoff's syndrome are 1) anterograde amnesia, 2) retrograde amnesia 3) severe memory loss 4) confabulation 5) meager content in conversation 6) lack of insight and apathy.

Unfortunately Korsakoff's involves neuron loss and damage to neurons. It then progresses to gliosis which damages to supporting cells of the central nervous system and can culminate into bleeding in the dorsomedial nucleus or anterior group of the thalamus (a very important brain organelle).

The damage is generally permanent and Thiamine treatment may help some, however it is more likely that the patient will need chronic care and a supportive living environment for the remainder of their life.

B is INCORRECT
Tardive Dyskinesia is characterized by repetitive, involuntary, purposeless movements, such as grimacing, tongue protrusion, lip smacking, puckering and pursing of the lips, and rapid eye blinking. Rapid movements of the extremities may also occur. The patient may also exhibit impaired movements of the fingers. People with Tardive Dyskinesia have difficulty not moving.

C is INCORRECT
Psychogenic fugue is an older term from the (DSM-IV Dissociative Disorders 300.13), and is a rare psychiatric disorder characterized by reversible amnesia for personal identity, including the memories, personality and other identifying characteristics of individuality. The state can be short-lived (hours to days), but can also last months or longer.
A type of psychogenic fugue is known as "dissociative fugue" which usually involves unplanned travel or wandering, and can result in the patient establishing a new identity. The amnesia remains for the period of the fugue state, but upon recovery, all

memories from the fugue state are usually integrated, into the overall memory.

D is INCORRECT
Alzheimer's disease is a newer name for a series of disorders which used to be called Dementia. Technically, the formal name of Alzheimer's is Senile Dementia of the Alzheimer's Type. It gets its name from the person who first described the symptoms, German psychiatrist and neuropathologist, Alois Alzheimer.

Question 164   Section: Clinical

The correct answer is B
Schizophrenia is a medical condition, which affects the brain. While we do not know its cause, and there is no cure, we do know (through MRI technology) there are significant changes in neuronal activity and there is often a significant loss of neurons. It is accepted, in the field, generally, that schizophrenia is the product of a disease process, or multiple disease processes and is not the result of internal psychological conflicts.

A is INCORRECT (Something you would want to focus on)
Anything you can do to preserve or maintain present levels of functioning is very important. Given the meager information presented in the question we have to make several assumptions. First, the client is not hospitalized, therefore they are living in the community. Second, they are functional enough they do not require hospitalization. Our goal should always be toward client self-determination and providing services in the least restrictive environment.

C is INCORRECT (Something you would want to focus on)
Any time you can orient a client to their present reality, whether they suffer from schizophrenia or another malady, you are

helping. A client who is reality focused can make better decisions regarding their life and future.

D is INCORRECT (Something you would want to focus on)
Working with adaptive behavior and helping the client make the behavior more adaptive is extremely important. Start where they are and lead them forward.

Question 165   Section: Clinical

The correct answer is C
The client has just used you as a movie screen and projected her mother onto you and is now transferring her emotions and desires onto the projection of her mother. As a therapist, you must withdraw the screen so the projection fails and therefore the transference is unsuccessful. This will cause the manipulation to fail and you should see the client attempt to use other mechanisms. Remember, the client is using this mechanism (set of behaviors) because it is very functional for getting their needs met. You have to assume that they are in therapy because they are running into situations where there old mechanisms no longer work as well, if at all. This is the time to explore and learn to use new mechanisms.

A is INCORRECT
Displacement is the mechanism whereby the user tries to reduce anxiety by "dumping" their feelings for one person (usually someone who has more power than them) onto another person (usually someone with less power than them.)

B is INCORRECT
A counter-transference reaction is identical in nature to a transference reaction, EXCEPT, it is the THERAPIST who projects and transfers feelings onto the CLIENT. Only the therapist can counter-transfer, and unless you are very aware

of what you are doing and are well grounded in psychoanalytic theory, counter-transference is usually BAD.

D is INCORRECT
Sublimation is an ego defense mechanism where a client has strong feelings on a specific issue and instead of expressing them, pulls them back inside themselves and uses the "ego" energy associated with the issue to power some other issue. This can be a very positive experience or it can be a very negative one. If you have strong feelings of being persecuted and treated unjustly, and you become an advocate for the less fortunate, channeling your "ego energy" into helping them battle injustice, this would probably be a positive example of sublimation.

Question 166   Section: Clinical

The correct answer is A
From age 6 to 12 a child is learning "methods of interacting" and "competence at interacting with others." This requires they learn to cope with their emotions. During this stage of development the goal is to create and develop new skills and knowledge. If we are allowed to do this, we develop a sense of "industry" or competence. Part of this stage is the development of control over our emotions, especially when dealing with other people. If the child fails to learn how to resolve feelings, they can develop a sense of inadequacy and inferiority. This will almost certainly damage self-esteem and competence. The parents are interfering with his ability to learn how to handle his emotions. Without an external outlet, he is likely to compensate for this lack of training in the form of internalized anxiety and fear.

B is INCORRECT

Eating disorders follow a similar path but there is no indication that there is a problem with food. It is possible, if this were a female instead of a male, they might begin to exercise control over themselves and their family, by controlling their food intact and /or binging and purging.

C is INCORRECT
Psychomotor problems are not usually associated with a compensation mechanism at this age. If you see psychomotor issues, it would be best to get a medical evaluation, preferably from a neurologist, immediately.

D is INCORRECT
Given the data in the question, this would not seem to be a problem, however, if this were to continue unabated, you might certainly begin to see this type of behavior by age 12 or 13. This boy will eventually learn to compensate for having their emotions squashed, but it will probably be a "non-productive" form of compensation.

Question 167   Section: Clinical

The correct answer is D
His approach is very intellectualized and rational. Alcoholism is a very complex illness that does not lend itself well to rationalization. Most alcoholics can rationalize their behavior or understand it as wrong, however, it is not often helpful to initial recovery. The reasons for his wife's alcohol problems could be physical/genetic, behavioral, psychological or a combination of all three. What is clear is he has taken on a co-dependent role and would benefit from working on codependent issues. You might also explore his familial background regarding alcohol abuse by his parents.

A is INCORRECT

His approach is a manifestation of denial and a refusal to see the complexity of alcohol abuse and addiction.

B is INCORRECT
This would probably not be appropriate for the initial stages of therapy. There are many issues, which would need to be met in order to deal with this specific issue.

C is INCORRECT
The "dance" between the ALCOHOLIC and the CO-DEPENDENT is very complex, subtle and reinforcing in ways that are almost never apparent. Both parties are getting needs met and both have agendas, whether understood of hidden. Alcoholism almost never "goes away" and his defense mechanisms could be adequate to last him the rest of his life without a change. An excellent text for understand the complexities of the alcoholic-codependent relationship is Claude Steiner's, "Games Alcoholics Play"

Question 168   Section: Clinical

The correct answer is B
Alcohol and drug addiction are extremely complex situations. One of the primary issues is life structure or lack of it. When a client is homeless or unemployed, they are lacking in structure. Boundaries, which are normally weak and unhealthy in substance abusing clients, are minimal or non-existent in this situation. There is no reason to look forward to a different day" and no concrete reason "Not to use."

A is INCORRECT
A concurrent anxiety disorder may well cause some problems with their addiction, however, it can be dealt with in treatment and does not necessarily correlate to a poor prognosis.

C is INCORRECT

Age does not correlate with poor prognosis. If anything, common sense would indicate that age would probably correlate with successful treatment. One of the tenets of substance abuse counseling is that you treat when you can and you treat every time someone comes back. It is not unusual for the addict to "fall off the wagon". Once they do and they come back to treatment, you pick up where they left off. They have a greater chance to absorb the lessons of treatment.

D is INCORRECT

It is a major mistake to diagnose or try to treat a personality disorder during an addiction. The basic concepts of addiction would indicate weak boundaries and poor ego strength. These are the hallmarks of both the addict and the individual with a personality disorder. Treat the addiction first and the "personality disorder" may go away, because it was never there to begin with.

Question 169   Section: Clinical

The correct answer is B

Cognitive behavioral therapy (CBT) is a psychotherapy whose aim is to solve problems of dysfunctional emotions, behaviors and thoughts through a systematic and goal-oriented procedure operating in the present. Empirical evidence exists that CBT is effective for treating a variety of problems, including mood, anxiety, personality, eating, substance abuse, and psychotic disorders. Treatment often consists of specific, technique-driven, brief, direct, and time-limited treatments for specific psychological disorders. It is useful in individual therapy and group treatment.

A is INCORRECT

Treatment's goal is to reduce the need for illegal drugs. There are many forms of treatment.

C is INCORRECT
This technique moves into the realm of insight-oriented therapy. This is usually done with a psychodynamic approach.

D is INCORRECT
This is generally done as a replacement maintenance therapy and its overall purpose is to reduce and eliminates the use of illegal drugs, as well as avoiding the criminality associated with drugs. When used as a treatment method for injectable drugs it reduces the transmission of infectious diseases and allows the user to gain health. This type of drug treatment is currently in use in the United States in the use of Methadone to treat Heroin, Morphine, Oxycontin and other opiate abuse.

Question 170 Section: Clinical

The correct answer is C
Of the numerous different Tricyclic medications current available all have an overdose possibility of increased cardiac toxicity. Of all of the TCA's, two of them (Elavil and Dothiepin) account for 81.6% of all the deaths by TCA overdose. When compared to all other drugs, TCA's are responsible for 34.14 deaths from overdose per one million prescriptions.

A is INCORRECT
SSRI's; selective serotonin reuptake inhibitors account for 2.02 deaths from overdose per one million prescriptions.

B is INCORRECT
MAOI's; monoamine oxidase inhibitors account for 13.48 deaths from overdose per one million prescriptions.

D is INCORRECT
Atypicals (Atypical antipsychotics) account for 6.19 deaths from overdose per one million prescriptions.

Reference
British MEdical Journal. 1995 Jan 28;310(6974):221-4.
Relative mortality from overdose of antidepressants.
Henry JA, Alexander CA, Sener EK.

Question 171 Section: Psychotherapy

The correct answer is D

During the initial phases of treatment, your client is likely to feel anger at the system and some hostility towards you as the treatment provider.   Just because the justice system has recognized that your client has a problem does not mean that your client has recognized his problem.   It would be unlikely that your client's behavior reached a level high enough to get the attention of the justice system without your client having a problem.

A is INCORRECT
Your feelings may well play a part in the initial phase of treatment.   They should not.   As you are only human, your feelings might interfere.   If they do, talk it out with your clinical supervisor.

B is INCORRECT
Everyone manipulates. It is human nature. Addicts attempt to manipulate more because they have a greater tendency to lie to themselves and therefore will lie to others. The disease of addiction fosters lying. As a counselor, you should expect it and then NOT take it personally.

C is INCORRECT

In court ordered treatment, the lack of local resources will not be likely to cause major problems during the initial phase of treatment. As the client begins to own their recovery and the response to their addiction process, then resource scarcity will play a larger part.

Question 172 Section: Ethics

The correct answer is A

This is a clear example of what ethics professionals call the "slippery slope". The chances of you accepting a cup of coffee as a token gesture will probably have no impact on your relationship with the client. But, you have just crossed a boundary, no matter how small, and the relationship has changed in ways that you can not predict. You do not know what "buying a cup of coffee means to the client"! In some cultures, providing food and drink is very important and sets up very clear roles. What happens the next time the client meets you and wants a cup of coffee but only has enough money for themselves. They then decide to forgo the coffee rather than embarrass themselves by not being able to but you one. Alternatively, they say, "Hey, I want a cup of coffee and I am broke today, since I got last time, how about you getting them this time?" Simple things can get complicated very fast when you do not maintain clear boundaries. Remember, boundaries are nothing more than rules you create about how to interact with other people. Make your rules and do not violate them and you will be much happier as a therapist.

B is INCORRECT

Nothing is "Just a …" All human behavior is rooted in needs. The client knows some of these needs and some are unknown and unconscious. Sharing food and drink is a rather intimate gesture. It is often a gesture among equals or among persons trying to start a relationship based on equality. The relationship between you and your client is never equal and never will be.

C is INCORRECT
This is an acceptable answer but not the BEST answer. By walking down to the cafeteria with them, they may perceive the relationship as more than therapist-client. If it is not a behavior you would do in your office with a client, then do not do it outside of your office.

D is INCORRECT
The moment you accept this offer, you have begun to change the boundaries of the relationship in very subtle ways. Whether you ultimately pay or not.

Question 173 Section: Ethics

The correct answer is C
This answer is the BEST answer given the choices and information given, however, information can only be released for specific reasons. Some of these reasons are: the client is being investigated for a crime involving sexual abuse or physical abuse of a child, elderly person, or a disabled person. Also, remember, you are never obligated to release any specific information to law enforcement, outside the boundaries of child/elder/disabled abuse without a court order. If you have any questions, always consult an attorney.

A is INCORRECT
Without informed consent, you cannot release to anyone. The rules regarding attorney-client privilege, and whether the information you have released falls under this protection is far too complicated for you to determine. If the client's lawyer wants information, get informed consent for the client before releasing it.

B is INCORRECT
NEVER...There is NO better explanation

D is INCORRECT
Definitely not! Just because you are married, and even if she is a clinician as well, you are not allowed to discuss your cases with your spouse.

Clinical Pearl: In the mid 90's my wife and I worked for the same private practice. I completed an assessment on a family; mom, dad and two sisters; and began seeing the youngest sister in individual therapy. I also saw the mom and dad occasionally in relation to the issues the youngest daughter was struggling with. Mom and dad told me they had gotten another therapist to see the older daughter. As per our ethics, I never questioned this. Three months after I began sessions, I was watching the 11 PM news with my wife and the face of my client, the youngest daughter, came on the news in relation to a serious crime having been committed. As I sat in shock my wife got up and said, "I need to call her mother and see how she is doing." I was confused, "Why would you call her mother? How do you even know the name of her mother?" My wife replied, "Because I am seeing the older daughter in therapy." To which I replied, "Funny you should mention that..."

My wife and I saw two different children from the same family in the same private practice and never knew the other was involved with the family. Just because you share a life, does not mean you need to share your work.

Question 174 Section: Ethics

The correct answer is D

This falls back on two very simple ethical concepts. The first – a Therapist-Client relationship is inherently one of different power levels. The therapist has more power and control than the client. The relationship is NEVER one of equals. The second – Once a client, ALWAYS a client. This is a boundary issue that you must adopt if you are to practice clinically. There are no exceptions. You can talk yourself into any situation you want and you can convince yourself that you are doing what is best or "there could be no harm", but, the truth is the possibility of harm exists.

A is INCORRECT
A written contract does not wipe away the concept of a dual relationship.

B is INCORRECT
Your feelings of a lack of an exploitive situation do not TRUMP the ethical code

C is INCORRECT
A dual relationship is a dual relationship, regardless of what you choice to discuss or avoid.

Clinical Note: I know these answers sound BLACK & WHITE...but boundaries need to be very clear. You are interacting with emotionally vulnerable people. You are simply a therapist, not a guru, sage or anointed person. You need boundaries...your client needs you to have boundaries.

Question 175 Section: Psychotherapy

The correct answer is B
Deceitful interactions and intentional destructiveness are both indicators that the family system would not be successful in family therapy. Family therapy requires commitment to change

and an overarching goal to make the group better than an individual. The pattern of deliberate destructiveness and deceitfulness are dynamics that an individual uses to maintain control in a pathological environment. These are "ID" based responses. This constellation would generally indicate there is no "SUPER-EGO" functioning of note in the family and therefore no shared purpose.

A is INCORRECT
The constant violation of interpersonal boundaries is a great place to start in family therapy. Families have many types of boundaries and many ways to mark their space. Interpersonal boundary violations indicate a system that needs "resetting" and "retraining". This situation is ripe for a family therapy approach.

C is INCORRECT
All families keep secrets. When the pattern become so pervasive it appears to dominate the clinical picture, it should be treated like a boundary issue. This situation is amenable to family therapy.

D is INCORRECT
Just because some members of the family have no desire to participate, if they show up they will probably benefit. The external pressure by the family will probably pull them into the therapeutic process.

Clinical Note: Family therapy is probably one of the toughest forms of therapy known to social work. Due to standard communication diagramming, you need to focus on so many variables in order to be successful, it is sometimes mindboggling. Social Work Programs offer a course in family therapy. You should definitely take it before attempting family therapy. But, if you want to be successful, you should also take several courses in the Marriage and Family Therapy program at your university. It also helps if you are slightly older and have your own family. There are unique issues to raising a family that will make you much more sensitive to a family's needs. If you wish to do family therapy, get "bunches" of training at every opportunity.

Question 176 Section: Psychotherapy

The correct answer is A
Enmeshment had a tendency to develop poor boundaries between people. It fosters a "poor ego strength" which can result in blurring between roles and responsibilities. This "blurring" between roles can be very devastating to a family.

According to Judith L. Herman in her 1981 book "Father-Daughter Incest." Published by Harvard University Press. She determined a number of 'markers' which would lead the therapist to believe there was a possibility of incest. Her study included 40 victims of father-daughter incest and 20 victims of non-contact sexual abuse.

She discovered that "incestuous families were conventional to a fault. Most were churchgoing and financially stable. They maintained a facade of respectability that helped hide the sexual abuse. The fathers' authority in the families was absolute, often asserted by force. Half of the fathers were habitually violent, but never enough to send a family member to the hospital. Their sexual assaults were usually planned in advance. The men were feared within the family but impressed outsiders as sympathetic, even admirable. In the presence of superior authority, they were ingratiating, deferential, even meek. They were hard-working, competent, and often very successful. Of the 40 fathers, 31 were the sole support of their families. Sex roles were rigidly defined. Mother and sisters were considered inferior to father and brothers. The incestuous fathers exercised minute control over the women's lives, often discouraging social contacts and keeping them secluded in the home. Most of the mothers were full-time housewives; six did some part-time work, and three had full-time jobs.

B is INCORRECT
Attitudes of permissiveness do not correlate highly with incest.

C is INCORRECT
Permeable boundaries and extreme chaos actually appear to correlate negative with incest. The incestuous family tends to be controlled, with rigid boundaries. Chaos seems to be the antithesis of incest.

D is INCORRECT
High conflict relationships tend to be negatively correlated with incest. This seems appropriate, as the severe violation which occurs in incest would require control and secrecy to maintain. A high conflict relationship would have a tendency to violate any secrecy and locus of control.

Question 177 Section: Psychotherapy

The correct answer is C
The client clearly suffers from a Major Depressive Disorder and the voices indicate some psychotic features are present. Remember, hearing voices or seeing things which do not exist are the hallmark of psychosis.
According to the DSM-IV:
> A) a person who suffers from major depressive disorder must either have a depressed mood or a loss of interest or pleasure in daily activities consistently for at least a two week period.

B) This mood must represent a change from the person's normal mood; social, occupational, educational or other important functioning must also be negatively impaired by the change in mood.

C) Major depressive disorder cannot be diagnosed if a person has a history of manic, hypomanic, or mixed episodes (e.g., a bipolar disorder) or if the depressed mood is better accounted for by schizoaffective disorder and is not superimposed on schizophrenia, schizophreniform disorder, delusional disorder or psychotic disorder.

D) Further, the symptoms are not better accounted for by bereavement (i.e., after the loss of a loved one) and the symptoms persist for longer than two months or are characterized by marked functional impairment, morbid preoccupation with worthlessness, suicidal ideation, psychotic symptoms, or psychomotor retardation.

This disorder is characterized by the presence of the majority of these symptoms:

>1) Depressed mood most of the day, nearly every day, as indicated by either subjective report (e.g., feels sad or empty) or observation made by others (e.g., appears tearful).
>2) Markedly diminished interest or pleasure in all, or almost all, activities most of the day, nearly every day
>3) Significant weight loss when not dieting or weight gain (e.g., a change of more than 5 of body weight in a month), or decrease or increase in appetite nearly every day.
>4) Insomnia or hypersomnia nearly every day

5) Psychomotor agitation or retardation nearly every day

6) Fatigue or loss of energy nearly every day

7) Feelings of worthlessness or excessive or inappropriate guilt nearly every day

8) Diminished ability to think or concentrate, or indecisiveness, nearly every day

9) Recurrent thoughts of death (not just fear of dying), recurrent suicidal ideation without a specific plan, or a suicide attempt or a specific plan for committing suicide.

A is INCORRECT

The Depressive disorder NOS category includes disorders with depressive features that do not meet the criteria for Major Depressive Disorder, Dysthymic disorder, Adjustment Disorder with Depressed Mood or Adjustment Disorder with Mixed Anxiety and Depressed Mood. Sometimes depressive symptoms can present as part of an Anxiety Disorder Not otherwise Specified. Examples include:

1) Premenstrual Dysphoric Disorder: in most menstrual cycles during the past years, (e.g., markedly depressed mood, marked anxiety, marked affective liability, decreased interest in activities) regularly occurred during the onset of menses). These symptoms must be severe enough to markedly interfere with work, school, or usual activities and be entirely absent for at least 1 week post menses.

2) Minor depressive disorder :episodes of at at least 2 weeks of depressive symptoms but with fewer than the five items required for Major Depressive Disorder.

3) Recurrent brief depressive disorder: depressive episodes lasting from 2 days up to 2 weeks, occurring at least once a month for 12 months(not associated with the menstrual cycle)

4) Post psychotic depressive Disorder of schizophrenia :a Major Depressive Episode that occurs during the residual phase of schizophrenia.

5) A Major Depressive Episode superimposed on Delusional Disorder, Psychotic Disorder Not Otherwise Specified, or the active phase of Schizophrenia.

Situations in which the clinician has concluded that a depressive disorder is present but is unable to determine whether it is primary, due to a general medical condition, or substance induced.

http://en.wikipedia.org/wiki/Depressive Disorder Not Ot herwise Specified

B is INCORRECT
The client clearly suffers from a Major Depressive Disorder, but the voices indicate a psychotic component which is not addressed in this diagnosis.

D is INCORRECT
The alcohol use occurred after the onset of the depression and became worse after the onset of the auditory hallucinations. The alcohol creates problems, but, was not the trigger or precursor to the problems.

Question 178

The correct answer is D
By far, the most serious potential for damage to children in substance abusing environments is neglect, physical and sexual abuse.

A is INCORRECT
These are not highly correlated with this family environment

B is INCORRECT
There have been no specific causal links in the research. If a person is "more prone" to develop Schizophrenia or Bipolar

Disorder may have increased problems due to the higher level of overall stress, however, no current correlation exists.

C is INCORRECT
Unfortunately, we have very little data on the causes of social phobia and panic attacks. They may be environment, genetic, or a mix of these and other things as well.

Question 179   Section: Psychotherapy

The correct answer is B
Both Substance Use/Abuse diagnoses and Mental Health issues are coded on Axis I. Only Mental Retardation and Personality Disorders are coded on Axis II. When a person suffers from a substance use/abuse disorder and a mental health diagnosis, they are said to have a dual (two) diagnosis and treatment becomes much trickier, because the entanglement of the two categories need to be teased out and sometimes you need to focus on the substance use first, and other times the mental health issues. This type of client is why you must get extra training in substance abuse issues.

A is INCORRECT
Neither of these issues would be coded on Axis II

C is INCORRECT
All Diagnoses are Multi-axial. They must cover all five axes.

D is INCORRECT
The DSM-IV-TR requires axial diagnosis.

Question 180   Section: Diagnosis and Assessment.

The correct answer is D
The purpose of the "Draw-a-Person" test is to assist professionals in inferring children's cognitive developmental

levels with little or no influence of other factors such as language barriers or special needs. Any other uses of the test are merely projective and are not endorsed by the first creator.

Test administration involves the administrator requesting children to complete three individual drawings on separate pieces of paper. Children are asked to draw a man, a woman, and themselves. No further instructions are given and the child is free to make the drawing in whichever way he/she would like. There is no right or wrong type of drawing, although the child must make a drawing of a whole person each time - i.e. head to feet, not just the face. The test has no time limit; however, children rarely take longer than about 10 or 15 minutes to complete all three drawings. Harris's book (1963) provides scoring scales which are used to examine and score the child's drawings. The test is completely non-invasive and non-threatening to children, which is part of its appeal.

To evaluate intelligence, the test administrator uses the Draw-a-Person: QSS (Quantitative Scoring System). This system analyzes fourteen different aspects of the drawings (such as specific body parts and clothing) for various criteria, including presence or absence, detail, and proportion. In all, there are 64 scoring items for each drawing. A separate standard score is recorded for each drawing, and a total score for all three. The use of a nonverbal, nonthreatening task to evaluate intelligence is intended to eliminate possible sources of bias by reducing variables like primary language, verbal skills, communication disabilities, and sensitivity to working under pressure. However, test results can be influenced by previous drawing experience, a factor that may account for the tendency of middle-class children to score higher on this test than lower-class children, who often have fewer opportunities to draw.

Reference: http://en.wikipedia.org/wiki/Draw-A-Person_Test

A is INCORRECT

Fine and gross motor function is best evaluated by an Occupational Therapist. This is usually not a social work function and you may be overstepping common practice, which could cause ethical issues.

B is INCORRECT
There would be no need to evaluate children's personality structures at this age. Personality is not fully developed and is malleable at this age.

C is INCORRECT
This test would not assess these issues. Some people have used it for this, however, it is not agreed upon to be tested or validated for it.

Question 181   **Section: Psychotherapy**

The correct answer is D
Your worker is suffering from compassion fatigue and is under tremendous stress. It may be totally related to the job or to other issues in her life; however, it is still a problem. Her productivity will decrease and you should expect to see problems with her judgment and scheduling. The initial method of addressing this issue is to give the worker time off and refer for stress counseling. The fact that this worker may need to change jobs or work in a different area of social work should also be considered.

A is INCORRECT
Counter-transference is a projection during therapy. The projection is from the therapist to the client. It is usually considered to be unhealthy and can be damaging to the therapist-client relationship as well as having the potential to create a dual relationship

B is INCORRECT

This worker may be depressed. The depression may have made her more susceptible to compassion fatigue, or may be a part of it. Regardless, the primary symptoms presented by the worker indicate burn-out, stress overload and compassion fatigue.

C is INCORRECT

There is no indication of projection occurring in the situation described by the question.

Remember, projection is a psychological defense mechanism where a person subconsciously denies his or her own attributes, thoughts, and emotions, which are then ascribed to the outside world, usually to other people. Thus, projection involves imagining or projecting the belief that others originate those feelings.

Projection reduces anxiety by allowing the expression of the unwanted unconscious impulses or desires without letting the conscious mind recognize them.

An example of this behavior might be blaming another for self failure. The mind may avoid the discomfort of consciously admitting personal faults by keeping those feelings unconscious, and by redirecting libidinal satisfaction by attaching, or "projecting," those same faults onto another person or object.

http://en.wikipedia.org/wiki/Psychological_projection

Question 182   Section: Psychotherapy

The correct answer is A

The Rogerian centered therapist uses current life events and reflects information back to the client in a "life-affirming manner." They are interested in the 'here-and-now' and will assist the client in 'being heard' so they can release the issues they are struggling with and be able to cope better and bring new and less problematic issues into their sphere of consciousness.

B is INCORRECT
Cognitive behavioral therapy (CBT) is a psychotherapeutic approach. CBT aims to solve problems concerning dysfunctional emotions, behaviors and cognitions through a goal-oriented, systematic procedure in the present.
The particular therapeutic techniques vary within the different approaches of CBT according to the particular kind of problem issues, but commonly may include keeping a diary of significant events and associated feelings, thoughts and behaviors; questioning and testing cognitions, assumptions, evaluations and beliefs that might be unhelpful and unrealistic; gradually facing activities which may have been avoided; and trying out new ways of behaving and reacting. Relaxation, mindfulness and distraction techniques are also commonly included. Cognitive behavioral therapy is often also used in conjunction with mood stabilizing medications to treat conditions like bipolar disorder.
http://en.wikipedia.org/wiki/Cognitive_behavioral_therapy

C is INCORRECT
The psychodynamic approach is interested in gathering information about current behavior and past experience to determine issues of developmental importance in the past and how to determine the impact of past issues on the present system.

D is INCORRECT
The multicultural approach is an eclectic system of many disciplines which focus on the role gender, culture, sexual-orientation and societal impacts affect the life of the client.

Question 183   Section: Behavior

The correct answer is B
Statistics are hard to come by and this appears to have roots both in the physical and the cultural. In general, adolescent males are more likely to act-out with aggression. This is probably related to the surge in testosterone (a male hormone) which comes around the early teen years.

A is INCORRECT

In general, girls are more prone to sexually acting out than boys. There appears to be multiple cultural and physiological issues involved in this answer, many of which are still being researched. Consider this a general interpretation of the data available.

C is INCORRECT
The data on this is very confusing. Some studies show girls more than guys and other studies show more equality between them (girl and guys run away at the same rate.)

D is INCORRECT
Once again the data is to muddles on this to be definitive. It would not be possible to say either sex has a higher prevalence rate.

Question 184   Section: Behavior

The correct answer is C
In psychoanalytic theory, the superego is a personality construct, which internalized the role of the parent. It can be viewed as the "parent inside your head" which helps you make decision which take into account the needs or feeling of others. It is believed to be created from having external parenting forces applied to the child during growth. The lack of this personality structure causes impulsive behavior, which does not take into consideration, the feeling of others.

A is INCORRECT

Ego functioning is simply the "adult role" during interactions.

B is INCORRECT
While the formulation of a conduct disorder may well be caused by a lack of a structured family system, the system is not a personality structure.

D is INCORRECT
Much like the answer to B, lack of an authoritative figure may help create an underdeveloped SUPEREGO structure; it is not a personality structure. The three Freudian Personality Structures are ID, EGO, and SUPEREGO.

Question 185   Section: Diagnosis

The correct answer is D
While it is age-appropriate behavior for children between the ages of four and six or possibly as late as seven to enter into a room nude in order to evoke some excitement, the fact that the child was found in a closet, indicates that they are interested in hiding their activity. The age of the child, the fact they were found in a closet with another child of the same age, and the fact that both children were naked, would lead you to consider that this is a sexually acting out behavior that has occurred because the child has been victimized. You would want to assess the child for possible sexual abuse victimization. If you were to get enough information to suspect victimization then you should report the incident to your local department of social services.

A is INCORRECT
An oppositional defiant disorder may possibly be diagnosed as early as age eight, it would require a lengthy list of behaviors which are problematic for childhood socialization.

B is INCORRECT
A conduct disorder is usually diagnosed in early to middle teenage years. A conduct disorder has marked examples of inappropriate, violent, and predatory behaviors.

C is INCORRECT
Attention deficit hyperactivity disorder is not generally associated with sexually acting out behaviors. The fact of the matter is, the sexually acting out behavior needs to be your issue of primary focus.

Question 186   **Section: Psychotherapy**

The correct answer is C
Displacement shifts sexual or aggressive impulses to a more acceptable or less threatening target.   This allows the redirection of emotions to a safer outlet and also allows the separation of emotions from real objects. The redirection of the intense emotion toward someone or something that is less offensive and/or less threatening, with the benefit of avoiding the issue   directly is very powerful. In this situation, she has displaced the sexual feelings she has for her ex-partner onto the new man in her life. It is safe to place them on him, while it is unsafe (due to rejection and emotional abandonment) to place her sexual feelings on her ex-partner.

A is INCORRECT
Distortion is the gross reshaping of external reality to meet internal needs. It is one of the pathological defense mechanisms. If a client is using this mechanism, you should be alert for severe pathology.

B is INCORRECT
Projection is a primitive form of paranoia. Projection also reduces anxiety by allowing the expression of the undesirable impulses or desires without accepting conscious awareness of them. It also allows the client to attribute his or her own unacknowledged, unacceptable and/or unwanted thoughts and emotions to someone else.

D is INCORRECT
Intellectualization is a form of isolation, which allows the client to concentrate on the intellectual aspects of a situation in order to distance themselves from the associated anxiety-provoking

emotions. They will use the mechanism to separate emotions from ideas; entertain desires and wishes in a formal and affectively bland manner in order to fail or refuse to act upon them avoiding unacceptable emotions by focusing on the intellectual aspects. This is a very difficult defense mechanism to counter in therapy.

Question 187   Section: Psychotherapy

The correct answer is D
In Gestalt Therapy, unexpressed guilt is viewed as unfinished business, which will cause the client to be unable to achieve a holistic, self-organizing tendency. In the gestalt perspective, the whole is greater than the sum of the parts. Unfinished business would be equated to focusing on a specific part of your life and being unable to integrate the rest.
Gestalt has two theoretical principles, which lead to two more methodologies, which it views as methodological principles. The Two theoretical principles are 1) Principle of Totality (The conscious experience is considered globally as it takes into account all of the physical and mental aspects of the individual, at the same time) and 2) the Principle of psychophysical isomorphism, which stated the existence of a correlation between conscious experience and cerebral activity.
From these two principles the two methodological principles are born. They are 1) Phenomenon Experimental Analysis – (from the Totality Principle, any psychological research should take as a starting point phenomena and not be solely focused on sensory qualities.) and 2) the Biotic Experiment – where the norm was experimenting in natural situations and under real conditions, that could be reproduces with greater fidelity in a habitual manner by the client.
This left Gestalt systems with four key principles.
1) Emergence, the process of complex pattern formation from simpler rules. It is demonstrated by the perception of the Dog Picture, which depicts a Dalmatian dog sniffing the ground in the shade of overhanging trees. The dog is not recognized by first identifying its parts (feet, ears, nose, tail, etc.), and then inferring the dog from those component parts.

2) Reification, the constructive or generative aspect of perception, by which the experienced percept contains more explicit spatial information than the sensory stimulus on which it is based.

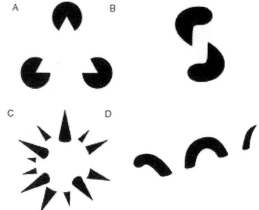

3) Multistability, the tendency of ambiguous perceptual experiences to pop back and forth unstably between two or more alternative interpretations. This is seen for example in the Necker cube, and in Rubin's Figure/Vase illusion.

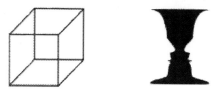

4) Invariance, a property of perception whereby simple geometrical objects are recognized independent of rotation, translation, and scale; as well as several other variations such as elastic deformations, different lighting, and different component features

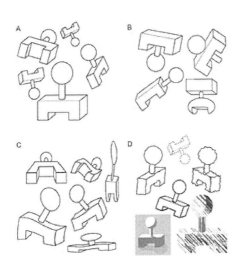

A is INCORRECT
Dysfunctional is too broad a term to accurately describe the situation.

B is INCORRECT
Unfinished business is never considered normal.

C is INCORRECT
Neurotic is an old term used by the psychoanalysts which has fallen out of favor with modern cognitive behavioral principles.

Question 188   **Section: Psychotherapy**

The correct answer is D
He meets the diagnostic criteria for an Antisocial Personality Disorder. He also meets the criteria for a conduct disorder, however he is over 18 now and the behavior has not stopped. A review of the diagnostic criteria follows:

(A)There is a pervasive pattern of disregard for and violation of the rights of others occurring since age 15 years, as indicated by three (or more) of the following:
(1) failure to conform to social norms with respect to lawful behaviors as indicated by repeatedly performing acts that are grounds for arrest (2) deceitfulness, as indicated by repeated lying, use of aliases, or conning others for personal profit or pleasure (3) impulsivity or failure to plan ahead (4) irritability and aggressiveness, as indicated by repeated physical fights or assaults (5) reckless disregard for safety of self or others (6) consistent irresponsibility, as indicated by repeated failure to sustain consistent work behavior or honor financial obligations (7) lack of remorse, as indicated by being indifferent to or rationalizing having hurt, mistreated, or stolen from another

B. The individual is at least age 18 years.

C. There is evidence of Conduct Disorder with onset before age 15 years.

D. The occurrence of antisocial behavior is not exclusively during the course of Schizophrenia or a Manic Episode.

A is INCORRECT
While he does meet the criteria for a conduct disorder, he has passed the age of 18 and the Antisocial PD is a more appropriate diagnosis. The criteria for a conduct disorder is:
(A) A repetitive and persistent pattern of behavior in which the basic rights of others or major age-appropriate societal norms or rules are violated, as manifested by the presence of three (or more) of the following criteria in the past 12 months, with at least one criterion present in the past 6 months:
> **Aggression to people and animals**
> (1) often bullies, threatens, or intimidates others (2) often initiates physical fights (3) has used a weapon that can cause serious physical harm to others (e.g., abat, brick, broken bottle, knife, gun) (4) has been physically cruel to people (5) has been physically cruel to animals (6) has stolen while confronting a victim (e.g., mugging,

purse snatching, extortion, armed robbery) (7) has forced someone into sexual activity

Destruction of property

(8) has deliberately engaged in fire setting with the intention of causing serious damage (9) has deliberately destroyed others' property (other than by fire setting)

Deceitfulness or theft

(10) has broken into someone else's house, building, or car (11) often lies to obtain goods or favors or to avoid obligations (i.e., "cons" others) (12) has stolen items of nontrivial value without confronting a victim (e.g., shoplifting, but without breaking and entering; forgery)

Serious violations of rules

(13) often stays out at night despite parental prohibitions, beginning before age 13 years (14) has run away from home overnight at least twice while living in parental or parental surrogate home (or once without returning for a lengthy period) (15) is often truant from school, beginning before age 13 years

B. The disturbance in behavior causes clinically significant impairment in social, academic, or occupational functioning.

C. If the individual is age 18 years or older, criteria are not met for Antisocial Personality Disorder.

Specify type based on age at onset:

Childhood-Onset Type: onset of at least one criterion characteristic of Conduct Disorder prior to age 10 years

Adolescent-Onset Type: absence of any criteria characteristic of Conduct Disorder prior to age 10 years

Specify severity:

Mild: few if any conduct problems in excess of those required to make the diagnosis and conduct problems cause only minor harm to others

Moderate: number of conduct problems and effect on others intermediate between "mild" and "severe"

Severe: many conduct problems in excess of those required to make the diagnosis or conduct problems cause considerable harm to others

B is INCORRECT
The behavior is to severe for an oppositional defiant disorder. Review the criteria below.
A pattern of negativistic, hostile, and defiant behavior lasting at least 6 months, during which four (or more) of the following are present:

(1) often loses temper (2) often argues with adults
(3) often actively defies or refuses to comply with adults' requests or rules (4) often deliberately annoys people
(5) often blames others for his or her mistakes or misbehavior (6) is often touchy or easily annoyed by others
(7) is often angry and resentful (8) is often spiteful or vindictive

> Note: Consider a criterion met only if the behavior occurs more frequently than is typically observed in individuals of comparable age and developmental level.

B. The disturbance in behavior causes clinically significant impairment in social, academic, or occupational functioning.
C. The behaviors do not occur exclusively during the course of a Psychotic or Mood Disorder.
D. Criteria are not met for Conduct Disorder, and, if the individual is age 18 years or older, criteria are not met for Antisocial Personality Disorder.

C is INCORRECT
Narcissistic Personality Disorder has an entirely different flavor. The criteria follow:
DSM-IV-TR 301.81 (in Axis II Cluster B) as: A pervasive pattern of grandiosity (in fantasy or behavior), need for admiration, and lack of empathy, beginning by early adulthood and present in a variety of contexts,

as indicated by five (or more) of the following:
(1) Has a grandiose sense of self-importance (e.g., exaggerates achievements and talents, expects to be recognized as superior without commensurate achievements) (2) Is preoccupied with fantasies of unlimited success, power, brilliance, beauty, or ideal

love (3) Believes that he or she is "special" and unique and can only be understood by, or should associate with, other special or high-status people (or institutions) (4) Requires excessive admiration (5) Has a sense of entitlement, i.e., unreasonable expectations of especially favorable treatment or automatic compliance with his or her expectations (6) Is interpersonally exploitative, i.e., takes advantage of others to achieve his or her own ends (7) Lacks empathy: is unwilling to recognize or identify with the feelings and needs of others (8) Is often envious of others or believes others are envious of him or her (9) Shows arrogant, haughty behaviors or attitudes

Question 189   Section: Psychotherapy

The correct answer is A
The Anchoring Bias is the common human tendency to rely too heavily, or "anchor," on one piece of information or one trait when making decisions. The client is more than their diagnosis and both sets of diagnoses may be wrong, skewed of inappropriate.

B is INCORRECT
The Attentional Bias is the implicit cognitive bias defined as the tendency of emotionally dominant stimuli in one's environment to preferentially draw and hold attention.

C is INCORRECT
The Bandwagon Bias is the tendency to do (or believe) things because many other people do (or believe) the same. Related to group-think and herd behavior.

D is INCORRECT
The Blind Spot Bias is the tendency to see oneself as less biased than other people.
Personal Note: It is my belief that given the expanded caseloads and lack of staff we, as social workers, have had to cope with over the past decade, it is very easy to become "sloppy" in our diagnosis. This can be related

to lack of time to correctly diagnose or just plain exhaustion. You should always come to your own diagnosis.

Question 190   **Section: Psychotherapy**

The correct answer is C
Normalcy bias – the refusal to plan for, or react to a disaster, which has never happened before.

A is INCORRECT
Negativity bias – the tendency to pay more attention and give more weight to negative than positive experiences or other kinds of information.

B is INCORRECT
Neglect of probability – the tendency to completely disregard probability when making a decision under uncertainty

D is INCORRECT
Omission bias – the tendency to judge harmful actions as worse, or less moral, than equally harmful omissions (inactions).

Question 191 Section: Diagnosis

The correct answer is D
While the precursor behaviors can be seen in early to late teenage years, it would be diagnosed as a Conduct Disorder. The DSM has an express prohibition for assigning a diagnosis of ASPD prior to the age of 18.
Antisocial personality disorder is characterized by a long-standing pattern of a disregard for other people's rights, often crossing the line and violating those rights.

Individuals with Antisocial Personality Disorder frequently lack empathy and tend to be callous, cynical, and contemptuous of the feelings, rights, and sufferings of others. They may have an inflated and arrogant self-appraisal (e.g., feel that ordinary work is beneath them or lack a realistic concern about their current problems or their future) and may be excessively opinionated, self-assured, or cocky. They may display a glib, superficial charm and can be quite voluble and verbally facile (e.g., using technical terms or jargon that might impress someone who is unfamiliar with the topic). These individuals may also be irresponsible and exploitative in their sexual relationships.

Symptoms of Antisocial Personality Disorder
Antisocial personality disorder is diagnosed when a person's pattern of antisocial behavior has occurred since age 15 (although only adults 18 years or older can be diagnosed with this disorder) and consists of the majority of these symptoms:

- Failure to conform to social norms with respect to lawful behaviors as indicated by repeatedly performing acts that are grounds for arrest
- Deceitfulness, as indicated by repeated lying, use of aliases, or conning others for personal profit or pleasure
- Impulsivity or failure to plan ahead
- Irritability and aggressiveness, as indicated by repeated physical fights or assaults
- Reckless disregard for safety of self or others
- Consistent irresponsibility, as indicated by repeated failure to sustain consistent work behavior or honor financial obligations
- Lack of remorse, as indicated by being indifferent to or rationalizing having hurt, mistreated, or stolen from another
  Reference: http://psychcentral.com/disorders/sx7.htm

A is INCORRECT

The diagnostic criteria for Childhood Disintegrative Disorder is presented below:

A. Apparently normal development for at least the first 2 years after birth as manifested by the presence of age-appropriate verbal and nonverbal communication, social relationships, play, and adaptive behavior.

B. Clinically significant loss of previously acquired skills (before age 10 years) in at least two of the following areas:
  (1) expressive or receptive language
  (2) social skills or adaptive behavior
  (3) bowel or bladder control
  (4) play
  (5) motor skills

C. Abnormalities of functioning in at least two of the following areas:
  (1) qualitative impairment in social interaction (e.g., impairment in nonverbal behaviors, failure to develop peer relationships, lack of social or emotional reciprocity)

  (2) qualitative impairments in communication (e.g., delay or lack of spoken language, inability to initiate or sustain a conversation, stereotyped and repetitive use of language, lack of varied make-believe play)

  (3) restricted, repetitive, and stereotyped patterns of behavior, interests, and activities, including motor stereotypies and mannerisms

D. The disturbance is not better accounted for by another specific Pervasive Developmental Disorder or by Schizophrenia.

B is INCORRECT
In children with this Pervasive Developmental Disorder there is substantial delay in communication and social interaction associated with development of "restricted, repetitive and stereotyped" behavior, interests, and activities.

Diagnostic criteria for 299.00 Autistic Disorder

A. A total of six (or more) items from (1), (2), and (3), with at least two from (1), and one each from (2) and (3):

(1) qualitative impairment in social interaction, as manifested by at least two of the following:

    (a) marked impairment in the use of multiple nonverbal behaviors such as eye-to-eye gaze, facial expression, body postures, and gestures to regulate social interaction

    (b) failure to develop peer relationships appropriate to developmental level

    (c) a lack of spontaneous seeking to share enjoyment, interests, or achievements with other people (e.g., by a lack of showing, bringing, or pointing out objects of interest)

    (d) lack of social or emotional reciprocity

(2) qualitative impairments in communication as manifested by at least one of the following:

    (a) delay in, or total lack of, the development of spoken language (not accompanied by an attempt to compensate through alternative modes of communication such as gesture or mime)

    (b) in individuals with adequate speech, marked impairment in the ability to initiate or sustain a conversation with others

    (c) stereotyped and repetitive use of language or idiosyncratic language

    (d) lack of varied, spontaneous make-believe play or social imitative play appropriate to developmental level

(3) restricted repetitive and stereotyped patterns of behavior, interests, and activities, as manifested by at least one of the following:

(a) encompassing preoccupation with one or more stereotyped and restricted patterns of interest that is abnormal either in intensity or focus
(b) apparently inflexible adherence to specific, nonfunctional routines or rituals
(c) stereotyped and repetitive motor mannerisms (e.g., hand or finger flapping or twisting, or complex whole-body movements)
(d) persistent preoccupation with parts of objects

B. Delays or abnormal functioning in at least one of the following areas, with onset prior to age 3 years: (1) social interaction, (2) language as used in social communication, or (3) symbolic or imaginative play.

C. The disturbance is not better accounted for by Rett's Disorder or Childhood Disintegrative Disorder.

C is INCORRECT
Children with this mental disorder, display repetitive nonfunctional movements that can result in bodily injury or interfere with normal functioning.

Diagnostic criteria for 307.3 Stereotypic Movement Disorder
A. Repetitive, seemingly driven, and nonfunctional motor behavior (e.g., hand shaking or waving, body rocking, head banging, mouthing of objects, self-biting, picking at skin or bodily orifices, hitting own body).

B. The behavior markedly interferes with normal activities or results in self-inflicted bodily injury that requires medical treatment (or would result in an injury if preventive measures were not used).

C. If Mental Retardation is present, the stereotypic or self-injurious behavior is of sufficient severity to become a focus of treatment.

D. The behavior is not better accounted for by a compulsion (as in Obsessive-Compulsive Disorder), a tic (as in Tic Disorder), a stereotypy that is part of a Pervasive Developmental Disorder, or hair pulling (as in Trichotillomania).

E. The behavior is not due to the direct physiological effects of a substance or a general medical condition.

F. The behavior persists for 4 weeks or longer. Specify if: With Self-Injurious Behavior: if the behavior results in bodily damage that requires specific treatment (or that would result in bodily damage if protective measures were not used)
Ref:
http://www.behavenet.com/capsules/disorders/autistic.ht
m

Question 192   Section: Diagnosis

The correct answer is C
The Global Assessment of Functioning (GAF) is a numeric scale (0 through 100) used by mental health clinicians and physicians to subjectively rate the social, occupational, and psychological functioning of adults, e.g., how well or adaptively one is meeting various problems-in-living. The scale is presented and described in the DSM-IV-TR on page 34. The score is often given as a range, as outlined below:
91 - 100 Superior functioning in a wide range of activities, life's problems never seem to get out of hand, is sought out by others because of his or her many positive qualities. No symptoms.

81 - 90 Absent or minimal symptoms (e.g., mild anxiety before an exam), good functioning in all areas, interested and involved in a wide range of activities, socially effective, generally satisfied with life, no more than everyday problems or concerns (e.g., an occasional argument with family members).

71 - 80 If symptoms are present, they are transient and expectable reactions to psychosocial stressors (e.g., difficulty concentrating after family argument); no more than slight impairment in social, occupational, or school functioning (e.g., temporarily falling behind in schoolwork).

61 - 70 Some mild symptoms (e.g., depressed mood and mild insomnia) OR some difficulty in social, occupational, or school functioning (e.g., occasional truancy, or theft within the household), but generally functioning pretty well, has some meaningful interpersonal relationships.

51 - 60 Moderate symptoms (e.g., flat affect and circumstantial speech, occasional panic attacks) OR moderate difficulty in social, occupational, or school functioning (e.g., few friends, conflicts with peers or co-workers).

41 - 50 Serious symptoms (e.g., suicidal ideation, severe obsessional rituals, frequent shoplifting) OR any serious impairment in social, occupational, or school functioning (e.g., no friends, unable to keep a job).

31 - 40 Some impairment in reality testing or communication (e.g., speech is at times illogical, obscure, or irrelevant) OR major impairment in several areas, such as work or school, family relations, judgment, thinking, or mood (e.g., depressed man avoids friends, neglects family, and is unable to work; child frequently beats up younger children, is defiant at home, and is failing at school).

21 - 30 Behavior is considerably influenced by delusions or hallucinations OR serious impairment, in communication or judgment (e.g., sometimes incoherent, acts grossly inappropriately, suicidal preoccupation) OR inability to function in almost all

areas (e.g., stays in bed all day, no job, home, or friends)
11 - 20 Some danger of hurting self or others (e.g., suicide attempts without clear expectation of death; frequently violent; manic excitement) OR occasionally fails to maintain minimal personal hygiene (e.g., smears feces) OR gross impairment in communication (e.g., largely incoherent or mute).
1 - 10 Persistent danger of severely hurting self or others (e.g., recurrent violence) OR persistent inability to maintain minimal personal hygiene OR serious suicidal act with clear expectation of death.

A is INCORRECT
This is coded on AXIS IV

B is INCORRECT
Provisional Diagnosis is coded on the AXIS it would go on if it was not a provisional diagnosis

D is INCORRECT

Question 193   Section: Diagnosis

The correct answer is B
According to Freud's psychoanalytic theory of personality, the superego is the component of personality composed of our internalized ideals that we have acquired from our parents and from society. The superego works to suppress the urges of the id and tries to make the ego behave morally, rather than realistically.
http://psychology.about.com/od/sindex/g/def_superego.htm

A is INCORRECT
According to Freud, the ego is part of personality that mediates the demands of the id, the superego and reality. The ego prevents us from acting on our basic urges (created by the id), but also works to achieve a balance with our moral and idealistic standards (created by the superego). While the ego

operates in both the preconscious and conscious, it's strong ties to the id means that it also operates in the unconscious. The ego operates based on the reality principle, which works to satisfy the id's desires in a manner that is realistic and socially appropriate. For example, if a person cuts you off in traffic, the ego prevents you from chasing down the car and physically attacking the offending driver. The ego allows us to see that this response would be socially unacceptable, but it also allows us to know that there are other more appropriate means of venting our frustration.

http://psychology.about.com/od/eindex/g/def_ego.htm

C is INCORRECT
The id is the only component of personality that is present from birth. This aspect of personality is entirely unconscious and includes of the instinctive and primitive behaviors. According to Freud, the id is the source of all psychic energy, making it the primary component of personality.

The id is driven by the pleasure principle, which strives for immediate gratification of all desires, wants, and needs. If these needs are not satisfied immediately, the result is a state anxiety or tension. For example, an increase in hunger or thirst should produce an immediate attempt to eat or drink. The id is very important early in life, because it ensures that an infant's needs are met. If the infant is hungry or uncomfortable, he or she will cry until the demands of the id are met.

However, immediately satisfying these needs is not always realistic or even possible. If we were ruled entirely by the pleasure principle, we might find ourselves grabbing things we want out of other people's hands to satisfy our own cravings. This sort of behavior would be both disruptive and socially unacceptable. According to Freud, the id tries to resolve the tension created by the pleasure principle through the primary process, which involves forming a mental image of the desired object as a way of satisfying the need.

http://psychology.about.com/od/theoriesofpersonality/a/persona lityelem.htm

D is INCORRECT

A term used by in psychoanalytic theory to describe the energy created by the survival and sexual instincts. According to Sigmund Freud, the libido is part of the id and is the driving force of all behavior.

The way in which libido is expressed depends upon the stage of development a person is in. According to Freud, children develop through a series of psychosexual stages. At each stage, the libido is focused on a specific area. When handled successfully, the child moves to the next stage of development and eventually grows into a healthy successful adult.

In some cases, the focus on a person's libidinal energy may remain fixed at an earlier stage of development in what Freud referred to as fixation. When this happens, the libido's energy may be too tied to this developmental stage and the person will remain "stuck" in this stage until the conflict is resolved.

For example, the first stage of Freud 's theory of psychosexual development is the oral stage. During this time, a child's libido is centered on the mouth so activities such as eating, sucking and drinking are important. If an oral fixation occurs, an adult's libidinal energy will remain focused on this stage , which might result in problems such as nail biting, drinking, smoking and other habits.

Freud also believed that each individual only had so much libido energy. Because the amount of energy available is limited, he suggested that different mental processes compete for what is available. For example, Freud suggested that the act of repression, or keeping memories out of conscious awareness, requires a tremendous amount of psychic energy. Any mental process that required so much energy to maintain had an effect on the mind's ability to function normally.

While the term libido has taken on an overtly sexual meaning in today's world, to Freud it represented all psychic energy not just sexual energy.
http://psychology.about.com/od/lindex/g/def_libido.htm

Question 194 Section: Diagnosis

The correct answer is D
The primary purpose of the DSM is to assess the client according to recognizable behaviors and symptoms as well as information gathered from the client and other collaterals.

A is INCORRECT
Given the wide variety of theoretical underpinnings utilized by our profession, there is no specific way to determine the "BEST" approach to treatment. As all clients are individual and respond differently, what may work for one person, may not work for another person. We do know that certain disorders respond better to specific kinds of treatment. For instance, Grief and Mourning responds better to group therapy, and Borderline Personality Disorder responds well to Dialectic Behavior Therapy.

B is INCORRECT
Mapping the etiology of a disorder may help us understand where it first developed and what stressors or life events have influenced it, however, it is not a function of the DSM.

C is INCORRECT
Evaluating a prior diagnosis comes from gathering information and reworking a diagnosis. The DSM is not specifically designed to assist in the evaluation of prior professional work.

Question 195   Section: Diagnosis

The Correct answer is D
Moderate Mental retardation is represented with an IQ range between 35-49.

A is INCORRECT
Borderline intellectual functioning is a categorization of intelligence wherein a person has below average cognitive ability (an IQ of 71–85), but the deficit is not as severe as mental retardation (70 or below). This is technically a cognitive impairment.

Clients in this range have a relatively normal expression of affect for their age, though their ability to think abstractly is rather limited. They tend to reason in a more concrete manner. They are usually able to function day to day without assistance, including holding down a simple job and the basic responsibilities of maintaining an apartment.

B is INCORRECT
Autism is a disorder of neural development characterized by impaired social interaction and communication, and by restricted and repetitive behavior. These signs all begin before a child is three years old. Autism affects information processing in the brain by altering how nerve cells and their synapses connect and organize. Autism is a spectrum disorder that does not necessarily correlate with mental retardation.

C is INCORRECT
Mild mental retardation indicates a person with an IQ range of 50-69

THE IQ SCALES ARE

Class	IQ
Profound mental retardation	Below 20
Severe mental retardation	20–34
Moderate mental retardation	35–49
Mild mental retardation	50–69
Borderline intellectual functioning	70–84

Question 196   Section: Diagnosis

The Correct answer is B
As a child develops, the process of internal monitoring sharpens and grows. This is the development of the superego. It is considered to be the controller of the human personality and allows the individual to judge things as "right" or "wrong". When a person has an under-developed or mis-developed superego, they are more likely to be impulsive and ego-

centered. They will want to meet their needs first, often without regard to the needs or wants of others. This impulsivity and "ME-centeredness" shows itself in many of the criteria of the Conduct Disorder.

A is INCORRECT

The function of the EGO is to moderate between internal impulses of the ID and with the help of the SUPEREGO, allow the client to interact with the world. This is the realm in which all of the ego-defense mechanisms can be used.

C is INCORRECT
An authoritarian parent is one who values control and power over discussion and cooperation. While you might think that imposing strict power and control over a child would assist the development of the internal moral control mechanism (Superego), it could actually hinder it if the child is not allowed to focus on and cope with his own internal controls.

D is INCORRECT
A rigid family structure is one with many boundaries and expectations. It may or may not be conducive to superego development, depending on the personality traits of the child.

Question 197   Section: Diagnosis

The correct answer is C
This is one of the Freudian stages of Psychosexual development.
"Fixation" is the Freudian term for problems with a stage. In this stage fixation can cause sexual unfulfillment, frigidity, impotence, and unsatisfactory relationships

A is INCORRECT
This stage is known as the Oral stage. Freud believed oral fixation might
result in a passive, gullible, immature, and manipulative personality.

B is INCORRECT
This stage is known as the Anal stage. Fixation at this stage
can take 2 separate paths. Retentive fixation might be
associated with obsessive organization or excessive neatness.
Explusive fixation might be associated with reckless, careless,
defiant, disorganized, and coprophiliac behavior.

D is INCORRECT
This stage is known as the Phallic stage. The major barrier to
overcome at this age is the Oedipus complex (in boys and girls)
according to Sigmund Freud.

Question 198   Section: Ethics

The correct answer is B
According to the NASW Code of Ethics, Section 1.08(a) :
Social workers should provide clients with reasonable access
to records concerning the clients. Social workers who are
concerned that clients' access to their records could cause
serious misunderstanding or harm to the client should provide
assistance in interpreting the records and consultation with the
client regarding the records. Social workers should limit clients'
access to their records, or portions of their records, only in
exceptional circumstances when there is compelling evidence
that such access would cause serious harm to the client. Both
clients' requests and the rationale for withholding some or all of
the record should be documented in clients' files

A is INCORRECT
There is no need to contact an attorney at this stage. You
could seek legal assistance from NASW, but knowledge of your
ethical code would probably be better.

C is INCORRECT
You cannot simply refuse to release the documentation, and
fail to follow-up with any other action.
D is INCORRECT
If you are concerned the content of the record may cause the
client a problem or that the content would need interpretation

by a professional to be properly understood, you can not
release the record.

Question 199   Section: Diagnosis

The correct answer is D
In 2000, the American Psychiatric Association revised the
PTSD diagnostic criteria in the fourth edition of its Diagnostic
and Statistical Manual of Mental Disorders (DSM-IV-TR)(1).
The diagnostic criteria (A-F) are specified below.
Diagnostic criteria for PTSD include a history of exposure to a
traumatic event meeting two criteria and symptoms from each
of three symptom clusters: intrusive recollections,
avoidant/numbing symptoms, and hyper-arousal symptoms. A
fifth criterion concerns duration of symptoms and a sixth
assesses functioning.

Criterion A: stressor
The person has been exposed to a traumatic event in which
both of the following have been present:
The person has experienced, witnessed, or been confronted
with an event or events that involve actual or threatened death
or serious injury, or a threat to the physical integrity of oneself
or others.
The person's response involved intense fear, helplessness, or
horror. Note: in children, it may be expressed instead by
disorganized or agitated behavior.

Criterion B: intrusive recollection
The traumatic event is persistently re-experienced in at least
one of the following ways:
- Recurrent and intrusive distressing recollections of the
  event, including images, thoughts, or perceptions. Note:
  in young children, repetitive play may occur in which
  themes or aspects of the trauma are expressed.
- Recurrent distressing dreams of the event. Note: in
  children, there may be frightening dreams without
  recognizable content

- Acting or feeling as if the traumatic event were recurring (includes a sense of reliving the experience, illusions, hallucinations, and dissociative flashback episodes, including those that occur upon awakening or when intoxicated). Note: in children, trauma-specific reenactment may occur.
- Intense psychological distress at exposure to internal or external cues that symbolize or resemble an aspect of the traumatic event.
- Physiologic reactivity upon exposure to internal or external cues that symbolize or resemble an aspect of the traumatic event

Criterion C: avoidant/numbing
Persistent avoidance of stimuli associated with the trauma and numbing of general responsiveness (not present before the trauma), as indicated by at least three of the following:
- Efforts to avoid thoughts, feelings, or conversations associated with the trauma
- Efforts to avoid activities, places, or people that arouse recollections of the trauma
- Inability to recall an important aspect of the trauma
- Markedly diminished interest or participation in significant activities
- Feeling of detachment or estrangement from others
- Restricted range of affect (e.g., unable to have loving feelings)
- Sense of foreshortened future (e.g., does not expect to have a career, marriage, children, or a normal life span)

Criterion D: hyper-arousal
Persistent symptoms of increasing arousal (not present before the trauma), indicated by at least two of the following:

- Difficulty falling or staying asleep
- Irritability or outbursts of anger
- Difficulty concentrating

- Hyper-vigilance
- Exaggerated startle response
-

Criterion E: duration
Duration of the disturbance (symptoms in B, C, and D) is more than one month.

Criterion F: functional significance
- The disturbance causes clinically significant distress or impairment in social, occupational, or other important areas of functioning.

Specify if:
- Acute: if duration of symptoms is less than three months
- Chronic: if duration of symptoms is three months or more

Specify if:
With or Without delay onset: Onset of symptoms at least six months after the stressor
> *American Psychiatric Association. (2000). Diagnostic and statistical manual of mental disorders (Revised 4th ed.). Washington, DC: Author.*

A is INCORRECT
A psychotic break describes a term used for an occasion when a person is experiencing an episode of acute psychosis. It could be for the first time, or after a significant period when the panic issue was in remission.

Environmental triggers, such as losing a loved one, are also known to be the precursor stressor prior to a panic attack. Some drugs have been associated with psychotic breaks. These include LSD, dextromethorphan (in higher doses), PCP, and opiates (mainly from experiencing withdrawal symptoms). There are other things can also cause temporary psychosis. Symptoms of psychotic breaks vary greatly, usually depending on the circumstances of diagnosis or any contributory substance ingested. Symptoms can range from harmless, sometimes unnoticed delusions, to violent outbursts and major depression.

B is INCORRECT
Panic attacks are periods of intense fear or apprehension that have a sudden onset[and of relatively brief duration. Panic attacks usually begin abruptly, reach a peak within 10 minutes, and subside over the next several hours. Often those afflicted will experience significant *anticipatory anxiety* between attacks, especially in situations where attacks have previously occurred. The effects of a panic attack vary.. Many who experience a panic attack for the first time, fear they are having a heart attack or a nervous breakdown. Repeated panic attacks are considered a syndrome of panic disorder.
 Screening tools like Panic Disorder Severity Scale can be used to detect possible cases of disorder, and suggest the need for a formal diagnostic assessment.

DSM-IV Diagnostic Criteria for Panic Attack
A discrete period of intense fear or discomfort, in which four (or more) of the following symptoms developed abruptly and reached a peak within 10 minutes:
- Palpitations, or accelerated heart rate
- Sweating
- Trembling or shaking
- Sensations of shortness of breath or smothering
- Feeling of choking
- Chest pain or discomfort
- Nausea or abdominal distress
- Feeling dizzy, unsteady, lightheaded, or faint
- De-realization (feelings of unreality) or depersonalization (being detached from oneself)
- Fear of losing control or going insane
- Sense of impending death
- Paresthesias (numbness or tingling sensations)
- Chills or hot flashes

C is INCORRECT
An adjustment disorder is a psychological response to an identifiable stressor or group of stressors that cause significant emotional or behavioral symptoms that do not meet criteria for anxiety disorder, PTSD, or acute stress disorder. The condition

is different from anxiety disorder because the anxiety disorder lacks the presence of a stressor, or post-traumatic stress disorder and acute stress disorder, which are associated with a more intense stressor. The DSM-IV identifies 6 types of adjustment disorders classified by their clinical features. Adjustment disorder may also be acute or chronic, depending on whether it lasts more or less than six months.

The diagnostic criteria in the DSM-IV are

A. The development of emotional or behavioral symptoms in response to an identifiable stressor(s) occurring within three months of the onset of the stressor(s).

B. These symptoms or behaviors are clinically significant as evidenced by either of the following:
1. marked distress that is in excess of what would be expected from exposure to the stressor
2. significant impairment in social or occupational (academic) functioning

C. The stress-related disturbance does not meet the criteria for another specific Axis I disorder and is not merely an exacerbation of a preexisting Axis I or Axis II disorder.

D. The symptoms do not represent Bereavement.

E. Once the stressor (or its consequences) has terminated, the symptoms do not persist for more than an additional six months.

Specify if:
- Acute: if the disturbance lasts < 6 months
- Chronic: if the disturbance lasts ≥ 6 months

Question 200   Section: Assessment

The correct answer is C

Always try to understand what the client heard and how they interpreted it. Therapy and assessment requires both people to constantly assess meaning and content of speech. Before you can do anything else, you should try to get the client to explain how they interpreted the previous statements. This will not only allow clarification but will empower the client by placing them in a situation where they have something of value (their interpretation) and you are asking for their help.

A is INCORRECT
The written policy would be a good step, especially of it is translated into Spanish, however, it is not the FIRST thing you would want to do and would likely alienate the client.

B is INCORRECT
It is generally good not to ask a "Why" question before you know the client very well. A "Why" question requires a client to defend a position or explain something they might not be fully aware of. This course of action could cause rather serious problems.

D is INCORRECT
This would not be your NEXT BEST move. If you did not have a social worker fluent in Spanish, you would be risking not providing services to the client of having them drop through the cracks. You should also remember this is an assessment and does not necessarily mean you will be providing long-term services. You want to ascertain what the client heard and how they translated the information. It is easy to misinterpret information during assessments and therapy.

17559039R00106

Made in the USA
Lexington, KY
16 September 2012